Learning Continuous Integration with TeamCity

Master the principles and practices behind Continuous Integration by setting it up for different technology stacks using TeamCity

Manoj Mahalingam S

PUBLISHING

BIRMINGHAM - MUMBAI

Learning Continuous Integration with TeamCity

First published: August 2014

Production reference: 1190814

Published by Packt Publishing Ltd.
Livery Place
35 Livery Street
Birmingham B3 2PB, UK.

ISBN 978-1-84969-951-8

www.packtpub.com

Cover image by Tony Shi (shihe99@hotmail.com)

Credits

About the Author

Manoj Mahalingam S is an Application Developer and Devops engineer at ThoughtWorks Inc., where he started his career five years ago. He mainly codes in C#, Python, and Ruby. He likes to think he knows Haskell, but *maybe* he doesn't. He is also extremely fond of PowerShell and is the author of the PowerShell-based build-and-release framework, YDeliver (`https://github.com/manojlds/ydeliver`).

He has employed Continuous Integration and Continuous Delivery in a number of projects, ranging across all the major tech stacks. He has also spoken at a number of conferences, including Pycon India and Devopsdays India.

He can be found answering questions on Stack Overflow at `http://stackoverflow.com/users/526535/manojlds` and also contributing to a number of projects on GitHub. He blogs at `http://www.stacktoheap.com`.

I would like to thank my wife, Gayathri, for supporting me and for helping me squeeze out the extra time needed to finish this book.

I would also like to thank my mother Mythili, my father Swaminathan, and my sister Priyanka for all their support and well wishes.

Finally, I would like to thank my employer, ThoughtWorks Inc., and also all my colleagues without whom I would not have had the knowledge and the experience to write this book.

About the Reviewers

Mark Baker is the Technology Lead of Tools at Mind Candy, home of the BAFTA-winning Moshi Monsters. His team is responsible for workflow and tools at Mind Candy and is dedicated to improving the quality of life for content creators and software developers.

Mark has been developing video games since 1998 and has worked for many game companies, such as Disney, Electronic Arts, and Sony Computer Entertainment, in a variety of roles, often concentrating on tools and infrastructure. He has contributed to multiple critically acclaimed games on different console systems. He has written a regular column on programming issues for the *Develop* magazine and presented papers at many industry conferences.

Evgeny Goldin is a Java, Groovy, and Scala developer who turned into a build, release, and deployment engineer to introduce order where chaos usually reigns. He's an open source developer, speaker, and passionate advocate when it comes to automation tools and techniques.

I'd like to thank my lovely wife, Inna Goldin, for giving her love and support and making this project happen.

Scott A. Lawrence is a software developer currently developing healthcare IT solutions in the Washington, D.C. metropolitan area. After graduating with a Bachelor of Computer Science degree from the University of Maryland, College Park in 1992, he's developed software solutions using Microsoft technologies for customers in various fields, including healthcare, marketing, e-commerce, as well as federal contracting for civilian and defense/intelligence agencies.

Eugene Petrenko is a passionate software developer and consultant. In 2009, he defended his PhD thesis in Computer Science. For more than 12 years, he has been working in many fields including .NET, Java, Windows APIs, server-side technologies, Spring Framework, Android, and Kotlin. He has been working for JetBrains since 2004. As a TeamCity team member, he has developed many core features. He has deep knowledge of the product and its internals. He is the author of several popular open source plugins for TeamCity, such as NuGet support, TeamCity.GitHub, TeamCity.Node, and TeamCity.Virtual.

Eugene also has a blog at http://blog.jonnyzzz.name.

www.PacktPub.com

Support files, eBooks, discount offers, and more

You might want to visit www.PacktPub.com for support files and downloads related to your book.

Did you know that Packt offers eBook versions of every book published, with PDF and ePub files available? You can upgrade to the eBook version at www.PacktPub.com and as a print book customer, you are entitled to a discount on the eBook copy. Get in touch with us at service@packtpub.com for more details.

At www.PacktPub.com, you can also read a collection of free technical articles, sign up for a range of free newsletters and receive exclusive discounts and offers on Packt books and eBooks.

http://PacktLib.PacktPub.com

Do you need instant solutions to your IT questions? PacktLib is Packt's online digital book library. Here, you can access, read and search across Packt's entire library of books.

Why subscribe?

- Fully searchable across every book published by Packt
- Copy and paste, print and bookmark content
- On demand and accessible via web browser

Free access for Packt account holders

If you have an account with Packt at www.PacktPub.com, you can use this to access PacktLib today and view nine entirely free books. Simply use your login credentials for immediate access.

Table of Contents

Preface

Continuous Integration (CI) has become mainstream in software development. Accordingly, the number of CI tools has increased as well. TeamCity by JetBrains is one of the leading CI tools available today, and it is suitable for small teams, large enterprises, and everyone in between. Being a flexible and feature-rich tool, it is also necessary to understand which features should be used, and which shouldn't, based on the specific context.

Learning Continuous Integration with TeamCity is a comprehensive guide to get started with CI, TeamCity, or both. With the goal of understanding CI and its benefits and utilizing TeamCity to realize the said benefits, the book uses sample projects and examples to explain how to set up CI. The projects are from the major tech stacks such as Java, .NET, Ruby, Python, Android, iOS, and more. The chapters also discuss the myriad tools in each of these ecosystems that are essential for a beneficial CI setup.

Every aspect of CI, the processes, tools, and the collaboration amongst the people is covered in terms of features offered by TeamCity. The book also takes a look at what's beyond CI—Continuous Delivery (CD)—and how TeamCity fares in setting up a fully functional CD setup.

What this book covers

Chapter 1, Introduction, discusses CI and its basic practices. The idea is to be on the same page when we discuss CI in the rest of the book and when implementing various solutions using TeamCity as a CI server. This chapter will also provide a high-level introduction to TeamCity, its features, and how it compares with competing products, such as Jenkins and ThoughtWorks's Go.

Chapter 2, Installation, discusses the installation of TeamCity, the server, and the agent. The aim of this chapter is to get started with a basic installation of TeamCity that can be used to configure and run the builds in the upcoming chapters.

Chapter 3, Getting Your CI Up and Running, comes up with a complete CI setup. We will start with a brief introduction to version control systems and the important role they play in CI. We will then pick up a sample project and set up CI for it. After getting a fully functional CI setup, we will explore some fine-tuning options that we have at our disposal. In the process, we will learn about the TeamCity terms, features, and concepts involved.

Chapter 4, TeamCity for Java Projects, covers the specific features that TeamCity provides for setting up CI for Java projects.

Chapter 5, TeamCity for .NET Projects, introduces the various tools present in the .NET ecosystem and also TeamCity's integrations with these tools.

Chapter 6, TeamCity for Ruby Projects, explains the various tools involved in setting up CI for Ruby projects. We will be covering RVM, rbenv, bundler, rake, and RSpec. We will also look at how these tools come together and integrate with features provided by TeamCity.

Chapter 7, TeamCity for Mobile and Other Technologies, explains how TeamCity fares when it comes to mobile projects, specifically Android and iOS projects. We will also look at some plugins for TeamCity and how they extend TeamCity to provide first-class support for even more platforms such as Node.js.

Chapter 8, Integration with Other Tools, teaches how TeamCity provides integrations with various tools, with the aim of making CI and interacting with TeamCity, a seamless experience.

Chapter 9, TeamCity for a Member of the Team, discusses how a user of TeamCity can take advantage of the features provided by the web interface of TeamCity to achieve various tasks that are expected of them in a CI setup.

Chapter 10, Taking It a Level Up, explains some of the more advanced concepts in TeamCity. These concepts can improve the entire setup of TeamCity and aid in moving towards a better CI setup.

Chapter 11, Beyond CI – Continuous Delivery, teaches us to expand on the concept and explores how a CD setup can be achieved using TeamCity. First, we begin by looking at what CD is and why it is beneficial. Then, we look at how the Deployment Pipeline can be configured in TeamCity so as to achieve these benefits of CD.

Chapter 12, Making It Production Ready, explains some of the steps needed to make our TeamCity installation ready for the real world.

What you need for this book

Depending on the tech stack/platform being used, a Windows/OS X/Linux based computer may be required.

For Java, a recent version of JDK 1.7 might be required. The .NET framework 4.0 will be needed for the .NET chapter.

Much of the installation of various tools and frameworks, including TeamCity, is covered in the book.

Who this book is for

Learning Continuous Integration with TeamCity is intended for teams and organizations comprising developers, testers, and operations and Devops, who are trying to start practicing CI, start using TeamCity, or both. If you have thought about bringing CI in to your team, if you are already using a CI tool and want to move to TeamCity, or if you are looking for ideal practices and techniques while implementing CI with TeamCity, this book is for you.

Since the book covers all major platforms/languages, such as Java, .Net, Ruby, Python, and even mobile, your project is most likely covered in the book.

Conventions

In this book, you will find a number of styles of text that distinguish between different kinds of information. Here are some examples of these styles, and an explanation of their meaning.

Code words in text, database table names, folder names, filenames, file extensions, pathnames, dummy URLs, user input, and Twitter handles are shown as follows: "An `init` script can be added and enabled for the agent, similar to the one for the server, in order to run it as a daemon."

A block of code is set as follows:

```
cover => coverage
nosetests.xml
```

When we wish to draw your attention to a particular part of a code block, the relevant lines or items are set in bold:

```
<project xmlns="http://maven.apache.org/POM/4.0.0" xmlns:xsi="http://
www.w3.org/2001/XMLSchema-instance"
   xsi:schemaLocation="http://maven.apache.org/POM/4.0.0 http://maven.
apache.org/maven-v4_0_0.xsd">
   <modelVersion>4.0.0</modelVersion>
   <groupId>com.stacktoheap.maven_ci_example</groupId>
   <artifactId>maven_ci_example</artifactId>
   <packaging>jar</packaging>
   <version>1.0-SNAPSHOT</version>
   <name>maven_ci_example</name>
   <url>http://maven.apache.org</url>
   <dependencies>
     <dependency>
       <groupId>junit</groupId>
       <artifactId>junit</artifactId>
       <version>3.8.1</version>
       <scope>test</scope>
     </dependency>
   </dependencies>
</project>
```

Any command-line input or output is written as follows:

```
wget http://www.trieuvan.com/apache/ant/binaries/apache-ant-1.9.3-bin.
tar.gz

tar xvfz apache-ant-1.9.3-bin.tar.gz

export ANT_HOME="~/Downloads/apache-ant-1.9.3"

export PATH="$PATH:$ANT_HOME/bin"
```

New terms and **important words** are shown in bold. Words that you see on the screen, in menus or dialog boxes for example, appear in the text like this: "If you choose to install the agent, next comes the **Configure Build Agent Properties** screen."

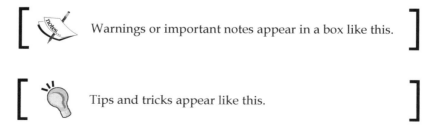

Warnings or important notes appear in a box like this.

Tips and tricks appear like this.

Reader feedback

Feedback from our readers is always welcome. Let us know what you think about this book—what you liked or may have disliked. Reader feedback is important for us to develop titles that you really get the most out of.

To send us general feedback, simply send an e-mail to feedback@packtpub.com, and mention the book title via the subject of your message.

If there is a topic that you have expertise in and you are interested in either writing or contributing to a book, see our author guide on www.packtpub.com/authors.

Customer support

Now that you are the proud owner of a Packt book, we have a number of things to help you to get the most from your purchase.

Downloading the example code

You can download the example code files for all Packt books you have purchased from your account at http://www.packtpub.com. If you purchased this book elsewhere, you can visit http://www.packtpub.com/support and register to have the files e-mailed directly to you.

Errata

Although we have taken every care to ensure the accuracy of our content, mistakes do happen. If you find a mistake in one of our books—maybe a mistake in the text or the code—we would be grateful if you would report this to us. By doing so, you can save other readers from frustration and help us improve subsequent versions of this book. If you find any errata, please report them by visiting http://www.packtpub.com/submit-errata, selecting your book, clicking on the **errata submission form** link, and entering the details of your errata. Once your errata are verified, your submission will be accepted and the errata will be uploaded on our website, or added to any list of existing errata, under the Errata section of that title. Any existing errata can be viewed by selecting your title from http://www.packtpub.com/support.

Piracy

Piracy of copyright material on the Internet is an ongoing problem across all media. At Packt, we take the protection of our copyright and licenses very seriously. If you come across any illegal copies of our works, in any form, on the Internet, please provide us with the location address or website name immediately so that we can pursue a remedy.

Please contact us at copyright@packtpub.com with a link to the suspected pirated material.

We appreciate your help in protecting our authors, and our ability to bring you valuable content.

Questions

You can contact us at questions@packtpub.com if you are having a problem with any aspect of the book, and we will do our best to address it.

1
Introduction

In this chapter, we will learn about **Continuous Integration** (**CI**) and its basic practices. The idea is to be on the same page when we talk about CI in the rest of the book and implement various solutions using TeamCity as a CI server. This chapter will also provide a high-level introduction to TeamCity, its features, and how effective it is when compared to competitive products such as Jenkins and ThoughtWorks' Go.

Introduction to Continuous Integration

Continuous Integration is the name given to processes and practices that are involved in regularly integrating the work of several developers into a shared mainline/repository.

My colleague Martin Fowler has written a popular article (`http://martinfowler.com/articles/continuousIntegration.html`) in which he defines CI as follows:

> "*A software development practice where members of a team integrate their work frequently, usually each person integrates at least daily, leading to multiple integrations per day. Each integration is verified by an automated build (including test) to detect integration errors as quickly as possible. Many teams find that this approach leads to significantly reduced integration problems and allows a team to develop cohesive software more rapidly.*"

Practices

There are some key practices that must be followed to have an effective CI:

- Developers check in code to a common version-control repository. This happens regularly, at least once a day. Everything—source code, tests, database migrations scripts, build and release scripts, and so on—that is needed to get the application running is checked in to this common repository.

- Automated builds run off the checked-in code. This is where CI servers such as TeamCity come into the picture. CI servers run automated builds whenever there are changes in the version-control repository. Every commit has to go through this process of automated builds.

- The builds include the process of testing the checked-in code. This includes running unit tests, code coverage, functional tests, and code inspection among others. All the tests must be cleared for the build to be certified as a fully *integrated* build.

- The automated builds should result in well-tested artifacts/binaries/ executables, depending on the type of the project. The artifacts must be easily available for anyone to download, and generally it is the CI server that provides the artifacts. In many setups, an external artifact repository such as Nexus or NuGet is utilized as well.

- The automated build process should be as quick as possible. The compilation, testing, and all the other steps to get the artifacts must be short to provide quick feedback.

- The automated process involved in getting the application running on a developer's box must be the same as the one used to run the CI.

- CI is about visibility. It must be clear what is happening to the builds and at what stage a particular commit is. Broken builds should be clearly highlighted and quickly acted upon. The CI server serves as a dashboard to this kind of activity. In TeamCity, users can quickly see the broken builds; the status of running builds and test failures, if any; communicate to the rest of the team that they are working on fixing a build; and pause the builds when needed.

- CI is also about team discipline. The team should ensure that broken builds are fixed as soon as possible and they never check in to a broken build. Developers must make sure that they run the build locally before checking in. Many of these can be attacked by technical solutions. For example, many VCSes allow the setting up of pre-commit hooks, which can be used to see whether the build is broken, and if so, prevent check ins. However, primarily, these are people's issues and have to be fixed appropriately.

- Automated deployments to a test environment against which we can run our automated functional tests is a key requirement in CI. The idea is to reuse the artifacts generated previously and deploy it into the environment without having to rebuild them again. The artifacts have to be agnostic of the environment they will be deployed into.

Benefits

CI brings a lot of value and benefits to the teams practicing it. Some of these include the following:

- Integrating code continuously leads to a more predictable and less tense integration process.

- Issues and bugs are identified and fixed earlier in the process. The presence of automated tests means that more bugs are caught as soon as a developer checks in the code. Also, it is inevitable that bugs escape the testing net. In such cases, the automated testing process that has been put in place encourages us to add tests so that similar bugs don't escape as well.

- One of the main benefits of CI is that you get reliable artifacts available to deploy at any point in time. The artifact has gone through lots of quality checks and can be deployed with more trust and less risk. This means that software can be delivered to the client/users frequently.

- CI encourages automation and helps in removing manual processes. As you build the foundation for automated tests and automated deployments as part of your CI, you are enabled to work further on this foundation and improve upon it over time.

Continuous deployment and Continuous Delivery

Continuous Delivery (CD) is the name given to the processes and practices through which applications are made available to be deployed into production at any time. CD is the natural extension to CI, which is more a developer team activity. CD is about making the built application ready to be deployed into production at any time. CD brings in the development team, the **operations (ops)** team, and the business together to ensure the application is released to production in a timely and appropriate way.

Continuous deployment is different from Continuous Delivery. The former is about deploying every build into production, while the latter is about making every build available to be deployed into production. The actual deployment depends on various business and ops factors, and hence not every build might end up being deployed into production. When we refer to CD in this book, we are talking about Continuous Delivery.

 CI can be seen as a subset of CD. The point where CI ends and where the parts that were introduced from the following CD begin is not clearly defined, and they can vary from one setup to another. It can be generally defined that CI ends with getting out the artifacts needed to deploy the application, and CD adds in the ability to deploy them into production in a reliable manner.

A key part of CD is what's called the build pipeline, which is what we will discuss in the next section.

The build pipeline

The idea of a build pipeline is to have your build process separated into various stages so that multiple builds can run at the same time. Each build can be in a different stage of the pipeline, thereby leading to a better throughput of builds.

A build pipeline helps to get fast feedback for the team. The first stage of the pipeline generally does the compilation to produce the binaries and runs the unit tests. The artifacts from this stage are passed on to the later stages. The first stage is expected to be very fast in order to provide quick feedback to the team.

The later stages perform various kinds of testing such as acceptance/functional testing and performance testing. These stages are generally slower due to their nature (for example, functional tests that hit the UI of the application are expected to be slower than the unit tests) and may be sequential or parallel depending on the requirements and/or resources available. The later stages also involve deployments to various environments such as the testing environment, against which we run the aforementioned tests, and **User Acceptance Testing** (**UAT**) environments that might be used for manual testing.

The pipeline will culminate in the deployment of the artifacts to production-like environments such as staging and eventually production itself. Not every stage of a build pipeline is automatically triggered. Deployments to most of the environments outside the environments used for automated testing are probably done manually as and when required. The following diagram shows a high-level view of a build pipeline for a project:

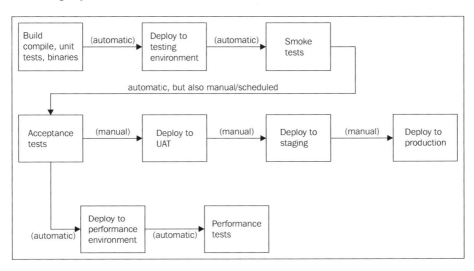

The build stage does the compilation, runs the unit tests, and produces the binaries. The binaries are then deployed into a testing environment for CI purposes. Quick smoke tests are then run to verify that the build is stable. Then, longer acceptance/functional tests are run. All the stages so far were automatic. The pipeline branches into a set of stages performing deployments to various environments such as UAT, staging, and production on one side, and, on the other side, a couple of stages performing performance tests after the pipeline is deployed into a performance environment. Deployment to various environments such as UAT is generally manual and is done as needed. The exact implementation of a build pipeline will vary from project to project and team to team. Typically, there are other dependencies such as libraries that come into the picture, but the overall structure should be similar to this.

The build pipeline, apart from aiding in fast builds and quick feedback, also enables you to ensure that only the builds that have gone through the rigorous testing process are finally deployed into production.

The build pipeline is also called the deployment pipeline.

Introduction to TeamCity

TeamCity is a CI server from JetBrains and comes with a lot of features out of the box to get you started quickly with CI for your projects.

As a CI server, TeamCity can detect changes in version-control repositories and trigger builds whenever new code is checked in. TeamCity can be configured to perform the build activities, which includes the compilation of source code, running unit tests and integration tests, deploying the built executables into a testing environment to perform functional tests, and exposing artifacts for downloads.

TeamCity is designed to help you follow the best practices of CI. With its ability to download artifacts from another build configuration, for example, TeamCity enables you to follow the approach of *build once and deploy everywhere*. TeamCity is feature-rich and flexible enough to allow you to follow the practices that suit your team and your needs the best.

This book will be using TeamCity 8.0.x, but we will also be looking at some of the newer features of the 8.1.x release.

Licensing

Before we get all excited about the amazing features that TeamCity brings to the table, it is worthwhile to explore the licensing options available. TeamCity is a commercial product from JetBrains, but the licensing options are designed so that small teams can get started with TeamCity for free.

TeamCity comes with the Professional Server License for free. It allows you to run a TeamCity server, which can have up to 20 build configurations, and use three build agents. In my experience, this is pretty sufficient for small projects. Teams can easily start their CI setup with TeamCity, and if they find a need for more configurations/ agents later, they can do so at that point in time. Additional agents can be bought separately, which also bumps up the maximum number of build configurations allowed by 10 each.

For bigger teams and projects, there is Enterprise Server License. This license enables you to have unlimited build configurations and agents with your TeamCity server. This also includes upgrades to the latest version of TeamCity for a year.

JetBrains also provides Open Source License, which is given for free to noncommercial open-source projects that qualify. This license is similar in features to the Enterprise Server License mentioned previously.

You can read up about the latest TeamCity licensing options at
`http://www.jetbrains.com/teamcity/buy/`.

Features

With the licensing options discussed, it's time to talk about the goodies that TeamCity comes with. As previously mentioned, TeamCity is feature rich. This section will focus on highlighting the most important features of TeamCity, especially with respect to the overall aim of setting up an effective CI.

First-class support for various technologies

TeamCity comes with great support for various technologies such as Java, .NET, Ruby, Android, iOS, and much more.

For example, if you have a .NET project that uses the Powershell-based PSake framework for its build, you can use the Powershell runner to run your build off a PSake build script.

The ability to support most platforms/technologies with very well thought out and first-class features make TeamCity a valuable tool to help you quickly get started with your CI setup.

Lots of plugins

This first-class and extensive support doesn't imply that TeamCity doesn't have or can't have plugins. It has quite a lot of them and for various purposes. Both JetBrains, and the community at large write plugins for TeamCity. Many of these plugins come bundled with TeamCity itself.

Many of these plugins are very useful and some of them are downright cool. A more recent plugin adds torrent abilities to TeamCity so that agents can download artifacts using the BitTorrent protocol, when appropriate.

A comprehensive list of available plugins can be found at `http://confluence.jetbrains.com/display/TW/TeamCity+Plugins`.

REST API

TeamCity comes with a REST API, which itself is a bundled plugin, that you can use to perform remote actions such as triggering builds, getting the status of running builds, and downloading artifacts among others. Depending on the particular requirements of your CI setup, the REST API can prove to be very valuable.

Comprehensive VCS support

As mentioned in the section where CI was introduced, **version control system (VCS)** plays an important part in CI. CI servers must support a wide range of VCSes, and must provide for flexible configurations that cater to the team's needs.

 We will be looking at VCSes in detail, and the role that they play in CI, in *Chapter 3, Getting Your CI Up and Running*

TeamCity supports almost every major VCSes such as Git, Mercurial, Subversion, CVS, Microsoft Team Foundation Server, and Perforce. TeamCity enables you to view the changes from the VCS for each of your builds and also provides high-fidelity diff views right in the browser. Triggering builds by looking at the changes in VCS can be fine-tuned to any extent. For example, you can avoid builds being triggered if changes happen within a particular directory in your repository, with other directories triggering builds as normal.

A nice dashboard UI and build history

Another important CI practice that TeamCity enables centers on the visibility and tracking of what is happening and what has happened. TeamCity provides a nice dashboard view of the projects and the build configurations in which builds are running, failing, and so on. The following screenshot of a TeamCity demo server gives a good view of the typical state of TeamCity's overview page:

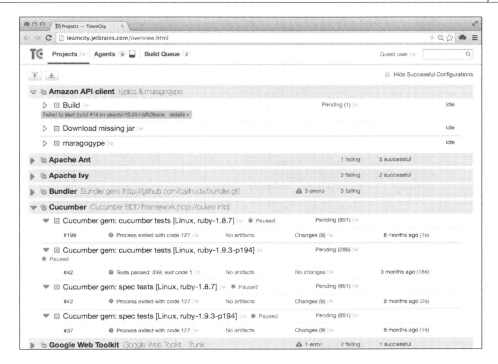

With user management features such as authentication and audit, it becomes easy to track who did what. A user can communicate, for example, if they are working on fixing broken builds. Other users can also assign people who are/have to investigate the broken builds.

TeamCity provides lots of features to track historical data of builds. With the help of statistical reports and graphs, you can quickly learn about the various characteristics of a build, such as build time and number of tests.

We can also set up and fine-tune how historical data is cleared up or preserved through the **Build History Clean-up** features. Builds that are promoted, to say production, can be pinned for eternity. Builds that ran a few days or even a few months ago (called history build) can be replicated, if needed.

Ease of setup and comprehensive documentation

All the features that TeamCity offers would be for naught if TeamCity makes it very difficult for you to make use of them. Thankfully, this is not the case. Getting started with your CI setup is a breeze with TeamCity. The configuration interface to set up projects and build configurations is straightforward. The main configuration items are clearly highlighted, and more advanced ones are available under the right levels of nesting.

TeamCity also provides features such as templates, a set of common settings from which build configurations can be quickly spawned that make it extremely easy for you to set up more and more build configurations.

The simplicity and power of TeamCity can be explained with one of my most favorite features. When you enable NuGet support in TeamCity, you can double up TeamCity as a NuGet repository feed by simply publishing the NuGet packages as artifacts; simple and intuitive!

TeamCity is also well documented and has a huge community of users around it. This makes it very easy for teams starting with TeamCity to make the right decisions when setting up their CI.

Build pipeline/chains

As mentioned previously, build pipelines are the ideal way to set up CI (and CD) for your projects. TeamCity has built-in support for such pipelining/chaining of build configurations.

Using the Snapshot dependency feature in TeamCity, we can easily configure build chains / build pipelines. TeamCity also comes with a nice visualization for build chains. The following screenshot shows one such build chain:

Agents and build grids

TeamCity comes with all the bells and whistles to manage a build farm or grid of agents. TeamCity makes it a breeze to manage tens, hundreds, or even more agents that may exist in the build grid. TeamCity can provide workload statistics, distribute load across agents, enable you to run builds on all the agents or only specific agents, and more. The following screenshot shows the Load Statistics Matrix of a demo TeamCity server:

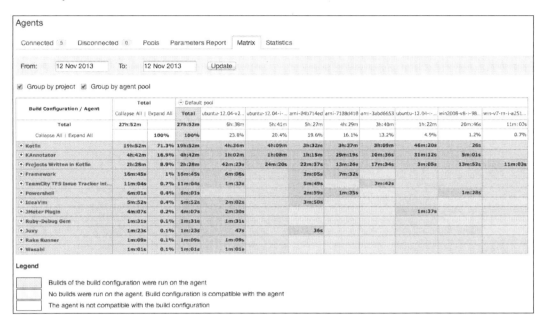

Also, with its Amazon EC2 integration, TeamCity can spin up VMs on EC2 and run the builds and bring them down as and when needed.

TeamCity doesn't even mandate all the agents to have the version control tool configured, as the server can do the checkout and send the files over. The server can also upgrade agents automatically.

IDE integrations

TeamCity has very well thought out integrations with various IDEs such as IntelliJ IDEA (another JetBrains product) and Visual Studio. Through the TeamCity plugins for these IDEs, it is possible to look at the status of the builds, the reason for the failures, and even trigger and pause builds without having to leave the comfort of the IDE.

Additional features such as precommit and personal builds are available through such IDE plugins.

The preceding set of features only scratches the surface of TeamCity. TeamCity has a lot more to offer. We will be exploring these and many other features of TeamCity in the coming chapters.

TeamCity and its competitors

TeamCity is a very popular and feature-rich CI tool. There are many other worthy CI tools as well, and it is prudent to compare TeamCity with these other tools. Here, we will be comparing TeamCity with Jenkins and ThoughtWorks' Go. The idea is to look at the biggest features of these two tools and compare them with those of TeamCity.

Jenkins

Jenkins (`http://jenkins-ci.org/`) is a very popular open source CI tool. It has a huge community around it and is used by many organizations and teams. The biggest advantage of Jenkins is its open source nature and the huge collection of plugins. There is a plugin in Jenkins for almost anything that you would want to do. With an active community around it, more and more plugins are added to tackle newer requirements.

What is probably the biggest strength of Jenkins is also its biggest weakness. To get any sort of work done with Jenkins, one has to install a multitude of plugins that interact in weird ways with each other just because they are written by different authors. To set up and visualize the build pipeline as described earlier, Jenkins will require the use of many plugins such as the Build Pipeline plugin, Build Name Setter plugin, Parameterized Trigger plugin, Copy Artifact plugin, Throttle Concurrent Builds plugin, and Promoted Builds plugin. That are a lot of plugins that you need to learn about and configure appropriately. It also doesn't help that there are many plugins to achieve the same thing, thereby adding to the confusion. With various plugins that need to work together, which were probably not tested together or even intended to work together, it becomes a pain to set up complicated pipelines with Jenkins. Not to say that complex setups aren't possible, but they could have been easier.

The following screenshot shows a sample build pipeline as visualized by the Build Pipeline plugin:

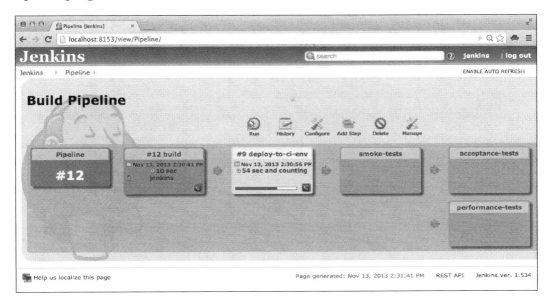

Jenkins is also not an ideal CI server for some platforms/technologies such as .NET. While there are some plugins available, there is not a whole lot of support for such platforms.

TeamCity comes with the right amount of bundled features to give you the feel that the platform of your choice is a first class citizen in your CI server. You also get the features needed to set up and maintain complicated pipelines, and just like Jenkins, TeamCity can be extended with plugins through its plugin API. As mentioned previously, there are a lot of plugins available for TeamCity as well, and many of these are open source too.

ThoughtWorks' Go

Go (http://www.go.cd/) is an open source CD/CI tool from ThoughtWorks Studios. It is a descendent of CruiseControl, one of the earliest CI servers. Go is available for free, with an option to buy commercial support.

 Go was a commercial tool but has been open sourced recently. The license terms for Go were very similar to that of TeamCity and allowed small teams to use Go for free.

Pipelines form the heart of Go. It has been designed with the build/deployment pipeline in mind, and as such, the visualization and configuration of pipelines is first class. There is no need to wire different stages of a pipeline manually, as they all fit together automatically. The following screenshot shows the pipeline visualization of Go in action:

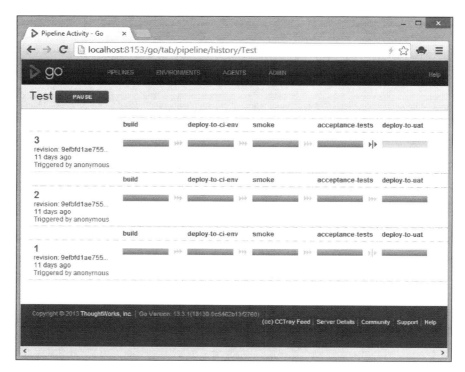

Go's plugin API is very limited and so is the number of plugins. The support for platform-specific task runners is very minimal at the moment. While all of the CI servers that we have talked about so far support the ability to run any arbitrary shell commands from the builds, it is good to have specific runners for specific tools. Having a Maven runner, for example, means that the setup is straightforward. One can specify the POM file, the goals, and other required parameters in the appropriate fields, rather than having to specify the exact command line in a shell runner.

In general, Go can be seen to have a limited set of features and doesn't provide a lot of flexibility. While tools such as TeamCity and Jenkins can be bent to meet our peculiar requirement, we might find that doing so with Go is not possible. This is mainly due to two reasons: the feature set of Go is small (but growing) and the developers of Go want the users to follow certain practices, hence restricting the options available. For example, in Go, templates can only be created for a pipeline. In TeamCity, we can create a template at the build configuration level (equivalent to a stage in Go).

The comparisons given here, obviously, aren't extensive but give you an idea about the most important advantages and shortcomings of the different tools. This can be seen as a starting point of your investigations into these tools.

 I work for ThoughtWorks, in the Professional Services wing. The product division of ThoughtWorks, ThoughtWorks Studios, makes Go.

Summary

In this chapter, we defined the practices and processes behind Continuous Integration and the benefits that it brings to the teams practicing it. We also had a high-level look at the build pipeline, which we will be using as the basis to set up CI for different technologies in the upcoming chapters.

The chapter also introduced TeamCity and its various licensing options, in addition to looking at the most important features that TeamCity brings to the table from the point of view of an effective CI implementation. We also compared TeamCity with a couple of its competitors to see how well it is placed in this space.

In the next chapter, we will look at the different ways of installing TeamCity on various platforms.

2
Installation

After introducing TeamCity and some of its major features in the previous chapter, we will take a look at installing TeamCity—the server and the agent—in this chapter.

The aim of this chapter is to get started with a basic installation of TeamCity that can be used to configure and run the builds in the upcoming chapters. Since the default packages come with both the server and the agent, the installation of these packages is sufficient to get started with a working setup. The instructions here are not meant for heavy production use. Please refer to *Chapter 12*, *Making It Production Ready*, for some pointers in that regard.

The installation procedures for Windows, Mac OS X, and Linux are written with some duplication. This is done so that those interested in only a particular OS have the option of reading only the corresponding section without having to refer to other sections.

Installing on Windows

Installing TeamCity on Windows is straightforward when using the setup package. The package includes both the server and the agent and provides the option to install either of them or both. The installation package can be downloaded from `http://www.jetbrains.com/teamcity/download/`.

TeamCity is a Java-based product and hence requires **Java Runtime Environment (JRE)**. The TeamCity installation package for Windows comes bundled with JRE 1.7 and the Tomcat 7 servlet container. This is recommended and is the easiest way to install TeamCity's server and agent on Windows.

Installing the server and the default agent

The steps involved in installing TeamCity using the installation package are as follows:

1. Double-click on the downloaded `setup exe` file. It should bring up the installation wizard like any other setup file on Windows. Accept the license and proceed to the next step.

2. The next step in the wizard is to choose the installation directory. This is where the TeamCity server (and agent) will be installed. The default directory is `C:\TeamCity`. We will be calling this `<TeamCity Home directory>`.

3. Since the package includes both the server and the agent, the next step asks you to choose the components to be installed. You can choose to install the server, the agent, and also choose whether Windows services need to be set up for each of these components. It is recommended that you set up the server and the agent as services.

4. Next, you will have to choose `<TeamCity Data directory>`. This is the path where TeamCity will store its configuration, build history, users, and other data. The default for this is `%ALLUSERSPROFILE%\JetBrains\TeamCity`.

Since `<TeamCity Data directory>` stores all of the data, including the artifacts, it is ideal to have this on a big enough drive, but not on the system drive. You can learn more about the data directory at `http://confluence.jetbrains.com/display/TCD8/TeamCity+Data+Directory`.

This step also sets the `TEAMCITY_DATA_PATH` environment variable to the path that you set in the wizard.

5. Continuing on, the installation copies the files and sets up TeamCity. The next bit of configuration that needs to be set is the port for the server. The default is `80`.

Port `80` may be used by other applications, including IIS, so it is not ideal to use this port, unless you definitely want to do so.

6. If you choose to install the agent, next comes the **Configure Build Agent Properties** screen. The following screenshot shows this screen for a typical installation:

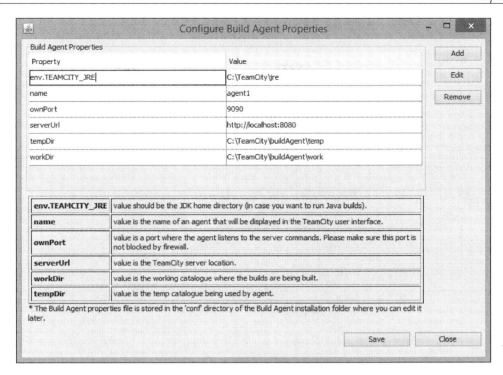

As seen in the previous screenshot, this screen allows you to view and edit various agent configurations. This includes the name of the agent, the port through which it communicates with the server, and the working directory of the agent. The defaults should be ideal for most setups. You may want to ensure that the firewall doesn't block the agent port (default 9090). These properties are saved at <Installation Directory>\buildagent\conf\buildAgent.properties.

7. If the server and the agent are being installed as Windows services, the next steps will ask you to choose between a local system account and a specific user account for them. It is recommended that you use a specific user with enough but limited rights for the services. The wizard also provides you with the option to start the services then and there. The user under whom the server service is running should have the following rights:

    ○   Write permission to <TeamCity Data directory>
    ○   Write permission to <TeamCity Home directory>
    ○   Right to log in as a service

8. The TeamCity web interface should open up with the **TeamCity First Start** page.

9. The first time installation asks you to agree to the license from the web interface, and you can opt to send usage statistics to the developers. You are also asked to set up the initial administrator account after which the TeamCity server should be ready for use.

 The steps are accurate for TeamCity 8.0.4. The exact steps may change in future versions, but the general process is expected to be the same.

Installing additional agents

Additional agents can be easily installed from the **Agents** page:

```
http://<serverUrl>:<serverPort>/agents.html
```

The **Install Build Agents** link at the top-right corner of this page can be used to download the agent installer (MS Windows Installer) directly from the server. The following screenshot shows the pop up that is presented once you click on this link:

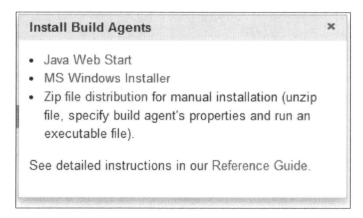

Installing an additional agent is very similar to installing the default agent using the combined installer, as described in the previous section.

Agents need to be approved from the **Agents** page. Agents on the same machine as the server are approved automatically, whereas any other agent must be manually approved for it to be added to the list of available agents.

Installation on Mac OS X

The TeamCity installation package (`Teamcity-<version number>.tar.gz`) can be downloaded from the download page at `http://www.jetbrains.com/teamcity/download/`.

TeamCity needs JRE or JDK 1.6+ to be installed. The recommended version is Oracle Java 1.7. It is ideal to have the JDK in case of the agent.

> The installation package is bundled with the Tomcat 7 servlet container. This is the recommended way to install TeamCity on OS X, unless you want to absolutely use your own installation of Tomcat or a different J2EE servlet container.

Running the TeamCity server and the default agent

The steps involved in getting an instance of the TeamCity server and agent up and running on OS X are listed as follows:

1. The downloaded installation package can be unpacked using a utility like **Archive Utility** in OS X. It can also be unpacked from the command line using the `tar` command:

   ```
   tar xvfz TeamCity-8.0.4.tar.gz
   ```

2. The package can be extracted, or the extracted contents can be copied over to the location where TeamCity is to be installed. Let's call this `<TeamCity Home Directory>`.

3. The `runAll.sh` script provided under the `<TeamCity Home Directory>/bin` directory can be used to start and stop the server and the default agent:

   ° To start both the server and the default agent, run the following command:

      ```
      <TeamCity Home Directory>/bin/runAll.sh start
      ```

   ° To stop both the server and the default agent, run the following command:

      ```
      <TeamCity Home Directory>/bin/runAll.sh stop
      ```

> The scripts in the `bin` directory may need to be marked as an executable using the `chmod +x bin/*.sh` command.

4. The `teamcity-server.sh` script can be used to start the server alone:

    ° To start the server, run the following command:

    `<TeamCity Home Directory>/bin/teamcity-server.sh start`

    ° To stop the server, run the following command:

    `<TeamCity Home Directory>/bin/teamcity-server.sh stop`

5. Once the server has been started, the web interface can be accessed at the default port, `8111`. This port can be changed by editing the highlighted section in the following piece of code from the `<TeamCity Base Directory>/conf/server.xml` file:

```
<Connector port="8111" protocol="org.apache.coyote.http11.
Http11NioProtocol"
    connectionTimeout="60000"
    redirectPort="8543"
    useBodyEncodingForURI="true"
    socket.txBufSize="64000"
    socket.rxBufSize="64000"
    tcpNoDelay="1"
    />
```

> **Downloading the example code**
>
> You can download the example code files for all Packt books you have purchased from your account at http://www.packtpub.com. If you purchased this book elsewhere, you can visit http://www.packtpub.com/support and register to have the files e-mailed directly to you.

6. The TeamCity web interface should present the **Teamcity First Start** page.

7. By default, `<Teamcity data directory>` is located at `$HOME/.BuildServer`. Setting the `TEAMCITY_DATA_PATH` environment variable can change it from its default value. The data directory location has to be chosen carefully as it stores all of the data, including the build history and the artifacts. More information on the data directory can be found at http://confluence.jetbrains.com/display/TCD8/TeamCity+Data+Directory.

8. The first time installation asks you to agree to the license from the web interface, and you can also opt to send usage statistics to the developers. The initial administrator account also needs to be set up at this point.

Setting up the TeamCity server as a daemon

The previous installation steps are helpful when you want to run TeamCity manually, using the scripts provided. If you want TeamCity to be set up as a daemon so that it can autostart once the system is restarted, you'll need to follow some additional steps.

The setting up of a server as a daemon is an advanced concept. The steps given here are representative, and they only highlight what can be achieved. The actual steps and scripts involved will be different for different use cases.

This section is optional and can be skipped.

The steps to configure the TeamCity server as a daemon are as follows:

1. Create a file named `jetbrains.teamcity.server.plist` at `/Library/LaunchDaemons` with the following content:

```
<?xml version="1.0" encoding="UTF-8"?>
<!DOCTYPE plist PUBLIC "-//Apple//DTD PLIST 1.0//EN" "http://www.
apple.com/DTDs/PropertyList-1.0.dtd">
<plist version="1.0">
<dict>
    <key>WorkingDirectory</key>
    <string>TeamCity Home Directory</string>
    <key>Debug</key>
    <false/>
    <key>Label</key>
    <string>jetbrains.teamcity.server</string>
    <key>OnDemand</key>
    <false/>
    <key>KeepAlive</key>
    <true/>
    <key>ProgramArguments</key>
    <array>
        <string>bin/teamcity-server.sh</string>
        <string>run</string>
    </array>
    <key>RunAtLoad</key>
    <true/>
    <key>StandardErrorPath</key>
    <string>logs/launchd.err.log</string>
    <key>StandardOutPath</key>
    <string>logs/launchd.out.log</string>
    <key>UserName</key>
    <string>Admin</string>
</dict>
</plist>
```

The XML content provides the configuration for the daemon. As it can be seen, the `ProgramArguments` key holds the script to be run and the parameters to be passed to it. We are using `run` instead of `start`, as `run` starts the server in the process, whereas `start` creates a background process. `WorkingDirectory` is set to `<TeamCity Home Directory>`. The logfile paths are also configured relative to `WorkingDirectory` using the `StandardErrorPath` and `StandardOutPath` keys.

The `UserName` key specifies the user the daemon should run under. Without this setting, it will run as the root (not recommended).

You can learn more about the `plist` file and the `property` keys at https://developer.apple.com/library/mac/documentation/Darwin/Reference/ManPages/man5/launchd.plist.5.html.

2. Once the `plist` file has been created, we can test that it all works by running the following command:

```
sudo launchctl load /Library/LaunchDaemons/jetbrains.teamcity.
server.plist
```

The preceding command starts the TeamCity server. We can look at the `launchd.err.log`, `launchd.out.log` and `teamcity-server.log` files under `<TeamCity Home Directory>/logs` to confirm that the server is running without any issues.

The following command can be run to stop the TeamCity server if needed:

```
sudo launchctl unload /Library/LaunchDaemons/jetbrains.teamcity.
server.plist
```

3. That's all there is to configure the TeamCity server as a daemon. The server should automatically start up the next time the system is restarted.

Installing additional agents

 The JRE or JDK 1.6+ is a prerequisite. (JDK is preferred for the agent since the agent may have to perform some build tasks that need the JDK.)

The steps involved in running additional agents on the same machine or on additional machines are as follows:

1. Additional agents can be easily installed from the **Agents** page (http://<serverUrl>:<serverPort>/agents.html).

2. The Install Build Agents link at the top-right corner of this page can be used to download the agent installer (**Zip file distribution**) directly from the server. The following screenshot shows the pop up that is presented when this link is clicked:

Install Build Agents   ✕

- Java Web Start
- MS Windows Installer
- Zip file distribution for manual installation (unzip file, specify build agent's properties and run an executable file).

See detailed instructions in our Reference Guide.

3. Unpack the downloaded archive and add it to the desired directory using the unzip command or the Archive Utility app. Let's call this directory <TeamCity Agent Home directory>.

4. Before starting the agents, the agent configuration properties have to be edited. The sample properties file, <TeamCity Agent Home directory>/conf/buildAgent.dist.properties, needs to be renamed to buildAgent.properties. In the file, the serverUrl property needs to be changed appropriately.

5. The default port for the agent is 9090. The agent must be able to communicate with the server on the server's port, and the server must be able to communicate with the agent on this default port.

6. Similar to the server and the default agent package, the startup scripts are located in the bin directory in <TeamCity Agent Home directory>. The agent can be started by running <TeamCity Agent Home directory>/bin/agent.sh start or <TeamCity Agent Home directory>/bin/agent.sh run. The former starts the agent in the background, whereas the latter will start it in the current console.

7. The agent can also be run as a daemon using launchd. The installation package comes with the necessary plist file, located at <TeamCity Agent Home directory>/bin/jetbrains.teamcity.BuildAgent.plist.

8. The `WorkingDirectory` property has to be changed to `<TeamCity Agent Home directory>`. The `UserName` property must be added and set with the user that the agent must run as, unless the agent needs to run as the root (not recommended).

9. The steps to install and test the `plist` file are similar to the server daemon's setup. Once the `plist` file is copied to `/Library/LaunchDaemons/`, the agent should start up automatically once the system is restarted.

10. Agents need to be authorized from the **Agents** page. Agents on the same machine as the server are approved automatically, whereas any other agent must be manually approved for it to be added to the list of available agents.

Installation on Linux

The TeamCity installation package (`Teamcity-<version number>.tar.gz`) can be downloaded from the download page of `http://www.jetbrains.com/teamcity/download/`.

TeamCity needs JRE or JDK Version 1.6+ to be installed. It is ideal to have the JDK instead of the agent.

> The installation package is bundled with the Tomcat 7 servlet container. This is the recommended way to install TeamCity on Linux, unless you want to absolutely use your own installation of Tomcat or a different J2EE servlet container.

We will be using Ubuntu 12.04 for the following steps. It should be straightforward to adapt it to the distribution of your choice.

Running the server and the default agent

The steps involved in installing a server and agent on a Linux system are as follows:

1. The downloaded installation package can be unpacked from the command line using the `tar` command:

```
tar -xvzf TeamCity-8.0.4.tar.gz -C /opt
```

The archive is extracted to `/opt` (resulting in `/opt/TeamCity`) using the preceding command.

> The scripts in `/opt/TeamCity/bin` may need to be marked as an executable using the `chmod +x /opt/TeamCity/bin/*.sh` command.

2. The `runAll.sh` script found under `/opt/TeamCity/bin` can be used to start and stop the server and the default agent:

   ° To start both the server and the default agent, run the following command:

      ```
      /opt/TeamCity/bin/runAll.sh start
      ```

   ° To stop both the server and the default agent, run the following command:

      ```
      /opt/TeamCity/bin/runAll.sh stop
      ```

3. The `teamcity-server.sh` script can be used to start the server alone:

   ° To start the server, run the following command:

      ```
      /opt/TeamCity/bin/teamcity-server.sh start
      ```

   ° To stop the server, run the following command:

      ```
      /opt/TeamCity/bin/teamcity-server.sh stop
      ```

4. Once the server has been started, the web interface can be accessed at the default port, `8111`.

5. The port can be changed by editing the highlighted section in the following piece of code from the `/opt/TeamCity/conf/server.xml` file:

   ```
   <Connector port="8111" protocol="org.apache.coyote.http11.
   Http11NioProtocol"
                   connectionTimeout="60000"
                   redirectPort="8543"
                   useBodyEncodingForURI="true"
                   socket.txBufSize="64000"
                   socket.rxBufSize="64000"
                   tcpNoDelay="1"
                   />
   ```

6. The TeamCity web interface should present the **TeamCity First Start** page.

7. The `<TeamCity data>` directory is located at `$HOME/.BuildServer` by default. Setting the `TEAMCITY_DATA_PATH` environment variable can change it. The data directory location has to be chosen carefully as it stores all the data, including the build history and the artifacts. More information on the data directory can be found at `http://confluence.jetbrains.com/display/TCD8/TeamCity+Data+Directory`.

8. The first time installation asks you to agree to the license from the web interface, and you can also opt to send usage statistics to the developers. The initial administrator account also needs to be set up at this point.

Running the TeamCity server as a daemon

The previous steps are good for running the TeamCity server (and agent) manually using the provided scripts. It is often necessary and convenient to have the server start up automatically once the machine has restarted.

 The steps given here are advanced and optional. This section can be skipped.

The following additional steps can be followed to set up a daemon for the TeamCity server:

1. Create the file /etc/init.d/teamcity-server with the following contents:

```
#!/bin/bash

USER=teamcity
BASE=/opt/TeamCity

SCRIPT=$BASE/bin/teamcity-server.sh

case "$1" in
    start)
    su -l $USER -c "$SCRIPT start"
    ;;
    stop)
    su -l $USER -c "$SCRIPT stop"
    ;;
    *)
    echo "Usage: teamcity-server start|stop"
    exit 3
esac
```

   The previous script is a simple init script for the server. This script allows you (and the system) to start and stop the server. The server is run under the teamcity user in this case.

2. Make sure that this file is made executable. This can be done with the following command:

```
chmod +x /etc/init.d/teamcity-server
```

3. The new init script needs to be enabled, which is done with the following command:

```
update-rc.d teamcity-server defaults
```

4. TeamCity server will now be started automatically once the system is restarted, and it will run as a daemon.

5. If needed, the server can be started and stopped by running `/etc/init.d/teamcity-server start` and `/etc/init.d/teamcity-server stop` respectively.

Installing additional agents

 JRE or JDK 1.6+ is a prerequisite. (JDK is preferred for the agent, since the agent may have to perform some build tasks that need the JDK.)

The steps involved in running additional agents on the same machine or additional machines are as follows:

1. Additional agents can be easily installed from the **Agents** page (`http://<serverUrl>:<serverPort>/agents.html`).

2. The **Install Build Agents** link on the top-right corner of this page can be used to download the agent installer (ZIP file distribution) directly from the server. The following screenshot shows the pop up that is presented once this link is clicked:

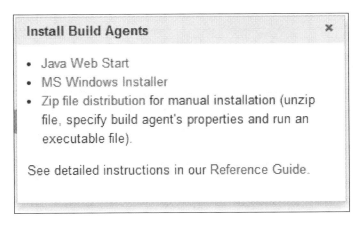

3. The `buildAgent.zip` package can be extracted to `/opt/TeamCityAgent` using the following command:

```
sudo unzip buildAgent.zip -d /opt/TeamCityAgent
```

4. Before starting the agents, the agent configuration properties have to be edited. The sample properties file `<TeamCity Agent Base directory>/conf/buildAgent.dist.properties` needs to be renamed to `buildAgent.properties`. In the file, the `serverUrl` property needs to be changed appropriately to point to the server.

5. The default port for the agent is `9090`. The agent must be able to communicate with the server on the server's port, and the server must be able to communicate with the agent on this default port.

6. Similar to the server and default agent package, the scripts to run the agent can now be found at `/opt/TeamCityAgent/bin`. The agent can be started by running `/opt/TeamCityAgent/bin/agent.sh start` or `/opt/TeamCityAgent/bin/agent.sh run`. The former starts the agent in the background, whereas the latter will start it in the current console.

7. An `init` script can be added and enabled for the agent, similar to the one for the server, in order to run it as a daemon.

8. Agents need to be approved from the **Agents** page. Agents on the same machine as the server are approved automatically, whereas any other agent must be manually approved for it to be added to the list of available agents.

Summary

Getting started with TeamCity is pretty straightforward on any platform, be it Windows, Linux, or OS X. This chapter covered the steps to get a basic installation of the TeamCity server and agent up and running.

This chapter did not cover the various settings and tweaks needed for a production installation of TeamCity, for example, using an external SQL database. There may also be changes to this basic setup due to build requirements. Such aspects will be covered in the upcoming chapters.

In the next chapter, we will get into the meat of this book—setting up CI using the TeamCity instance that we have just set up.

3
Getting Your CI Up and Running

With our basic TeamCity setup done, in this chapter, we will aim to come up with a complete CI setup. The chapter will start with a brief introduction to version control systems and the important role they play in CI.

We will then pick up a sample project and set up CI for it. When we have a fully functional CI setup, we will explore some fine-tuning options that we have at our disposal. In the process, you will learn about the TeamCity terms, features, and concepts involved.

Introducing version control systems

Version control systems (**VCSs**) help us to record and track changes to files. Most often, the files that are being tracked are source code files, but they could in reality be any kind of file imaginable. With VCSs, we can look back at all the changes made to a file (or set of files) and who performed them. We can move back to a particular revision if we find a problem with the current one and also pinpoint who caused it. VCSs are also called revision control systems, configuration management tools, and source code manager.

Centralized versus distributed VCSs

Early examples of VCSs were CVS and **Subversion** (**SVN**). These are now known as centralized VCSs. In the past, there was a centralized server where several clients checked out code and checked them in after necessary changes were made. In such a system, the server was the single source of truth and also the single point of failure.

More recently, another breed of VCSs has emerged. These are distributed VCSs, with the prime examples being Git and Mercurial (Hg). The primary distinguishing feature of DVCSs is that everyone working on the code contained in the repository has a copy of the entire repository and not just a snapshot of it. That is, the actual files that are being worked on and the complete metadata that is used to track the changes to these files are part of every checkout. Since everyone has a full repository, there is no single point of failure. In many DVCS setups, there is a single *blessed* repository that everyone else pushes to. In this, it may seem like a centralized setup, such as CVS and Subversion, but client repositories can collaborate with each other too if required.

VCSs and CI

As mentioned in *Chapter 1, Introduction*, when CI was introduced, VCSs are an integral part of CI. One of the first things that needs to be set up for a proper CI is a single version control system where everything that is required to build the software is put. A source repository should be set up in such a way that a simple checkout should be enough to build the software. It is against the source code that is contained in the VCS that we run our CI builds using a CI tool like TeamCity.

VCSs are not only integral to CI, but they ought to be integral to any software development, even if it is a simple pet project that is being coded by burning the midnight oil.

VCSs provide you with the safety net needed to go back from a broken state to a state that was known to work. They also provide you with the complete revision history of your source code, enabling you to track changes to different parts of your codebase. If you are keeping multiple copies of files/ directories as you make changes, you are already doing some kind of rudimentary version control.

VCS used in this book

Git has become very popular in recent years, especially for open source development. Platforms such as GitHub have made it even more popular. Though TeamCity has excellent support for all the VCSs that you could end up using in your projects, in this book the examples and setup instructions will mainly concentrate on using Git as the VCS. Using a VCS of your choice instead of Git with TeamCity should be straightforward.

GitHub (`https://github.com/`) is a social platform for coders. It offers source code hosting for individuals and teams. As the name suggests, Git is the VCS of choice at GitHub. Open source projects can be hosted and collaborated on GitHub for free, whereas private repositories can be paid for and obtained. Bitbucket (`https://bitbucket.org/`) is a similar service, which started off with Mercurial as its VCS, but has added Git support as well. There are options to host Git repositories in-house and get features similar to GitHub and Bitbucket as well, with GitLab (`http://gitlab.org/`) being one of them.

GitHub provides a very detailed tutorial (`https://help.github.com/articles/set-up-git`) on getting started with Git and GitHub for all major platforms.

Setting up CI

In the rest of the chapter, we will go about setting up CI for a simple sample project. While setting up the CI for the sample project, we will be going through the TeamCity concepts and configuration involved in detail. The idea is to concentrate on the configuration aspect and not on the technology stack of the sample project itself.

The sample project

We will be using a simple Django application as the sample project for this chapter. As previously mentioned, the project is maintained in a Git repository and is hosted on GitHub at `https://github.com/manojlds/django_ci_example`.

Django is a Python-based MVC framework to build websites and web applications. I chose a Django project as the sample project for this chapter due to its simplicity, good documentation and tutorials, and most importantly because I am a huge fan of Django and Python. More information about the Django framework can be found at `https://www.djangoproject.com/`.

We will be setting up the complete CI for this project. The aim is to come up with a simple build pipeline as described in the first chapter but also cover the CI aspect more than the deployment and Continuous Delivery aspects. The simple build pipeline will perform basic error checking and style checking on the code and run unit tests. If these pass, the next stage will deploy the application to a test environment, after which we will run a suite of functional tests against this deployed instance. Every check-in will have to go through all these steps to be deemed fully integrated with the mainline.

This chapter does not go deeply into the concepts behind Django or the tools involved, and instead keeps things at a very high level. The techniques applied and the overall CI setup will be similar for other projects. Various setup activities such as database setup for the application, installing dependencies, and others, are not explained in detail to keep the chapter focused on the TeamCity concepts.

Refer to the README for the django_ci_example project located at h

Creating a project in TeamCity

When we visit the TeamCity overview page after finishing all the installation steps as mentioned in *Chapter 2, Installation*, the most prominent thing that we will be asked to do is to create a project.

A project is a logical grouping of builds that you want to run as part of the CI for your team/organization. What a TeamCity project translates to—a collection of builds for a single software product, builds of a VCS branch of the said product, or a collection of deployment jobs to various servers in production—is going to vary from project to project even within the same team/organization.

The first step in starting to configure a TeamCity server to run builds, and hence CI, is to create the necessary project. Clicking on the **Create project** link takes us to the **Create New Project** page where we can create our project by providing a suitable name and an optional description for it, as can be seen in the following screenshot:

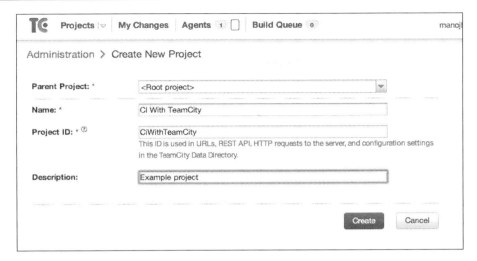

 The ID for a project, and most other entities within TeamCity, is automatically generated when the entity is created. The ID is used to uniquely identify the entity in TeamCity URLs and API calls, among others. It is preferable to use the generated ID rather than change it, as TeamCity generates IDs that follow consistent conventions across the server. However, changing IDs might be useful when you have to move entities to a different server where the same IDs may already exist.

We can create the project that we need by clicking on the **Create** button. Once the project is created, we are taken to the project configuration page, where we can add subprojects, build configurations, VCS roots, and more. These TeamCity entities will be explained in the coming pages.

Subprojects

TeamCity projects can themselves contain other projects. Subprojects are useful for hierarchical display and classification of builds, and also help in easily configuring and sharing similar settings and entities across projects. One use case of subprojects is to have subprojects for each branch/release version of a code base.

 The root project is a special project that is the parent of every project and is automatically created. Furthermore, it cannot be deleted or have any build configurations of its own. The main purpose of the root project is to create and maintain settings and entities (such as VCS roots) for use by all projects in the server.

Adding build configurations

Build configurations in TeamCity are a collection of tasks that make a build, along with the settings needed to describe where the build fetches the source code from, when it runs, and what artifacts it produces.

For our sample project, we will begin by adding a build configuration named `build`. This build configuration will perform build activities such as checking the code for errors and running unit tests and coverage.

From the project configuration page for the project we created previously, click on the **Create Build Configuration** button to add a build configuration to the project. The following screenshot shows a typical build configuration creation page:

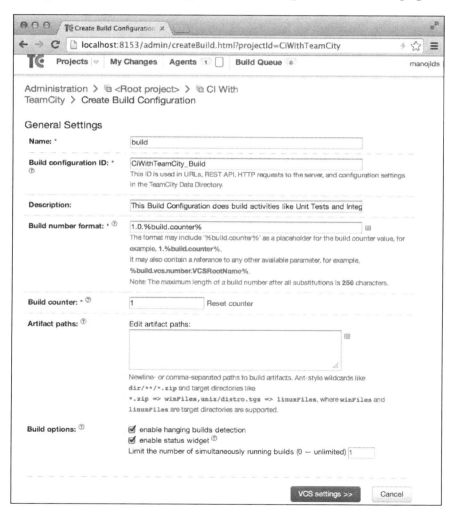

The **Name**, **Build configuration ID**, and **Description** settings are pretty straightforward and are similar to those of projects. A brief explanation of each of these settings is given as follows:

- The **Build number format** setting is used to specify the format in which the build number for each build of this build configuration is to be recorded. The exact format will depend on the type of project and/or organizational/team conventions. Some teams include plain build counters, while some teams also include the VCS `changeset` information in the build numbers. TeamCity has the ability to specify various parameters in this field (and elsewhere) that provide such information. The default `%build.counter%` parameter that is seen when creating a build configuration is one such parameter.

- We will follow semantic versioning in this book (`http://semver.org/`). It prescribes version numbers to be in the format MAJOR.MINOR.PATCH. For example, the numbers may look like `1.0.25`, `2.1.567`, and so on. Following this format of version numbers, we will set the **Build number format** as `1.0.%build.counter%`.

- The **Build counter** setting is used to set or reset the internal build counter that TeamCity maintains for this build. We don't have to change this now (from the default `1`.) This is useful when we want to change the MAJOR version number, say, from `1.0.x` to `2.0.x`, and hence, would want to start counting builds from 1 again.

- The **Artifact paths** setting is used to configure the paths from which artifacts have to be uploaded for this build. TeamCity's artifact management process is such that the generated files and folders in an agent during a build process can be marked as artifacts using this setting. These files are uploaded back to the TeamCity server and exposed via the web interface as artifacts. Any other build configuration that is dependent on this particular build configuration can fetch and use these artifacts as needed. We will come back to configuring and using artifacts in a later section and leave this setting empty for now.

- There are three **Build options** that can be set up as desired.

  - **Hanging builds detection** can be enabled if we want TeamCity to detect and stop build configurations that have been running for a long time—longer than their usual runtime—and not providing any messages back to TeamCity.

- ° The **Status widget** can be enabled to make build configuration information available through various APIs. For example, **Build monitors** can generally access the status of a build configuration only if this setting is enabled. It is recommended to enable both these settings as they are highly useful.

- ° For the **Limit the number of simultaneously running builds (0 - unlimited)** setting, it is recommended to set a value of 1. This means that at any point in time, only one instance of this build configuration will run, which is what we require for our CI setup. Setting a positive integer n means that n number of instances of this build configuration will run (in n agents.) Setting it to 0 will allow for a potentially unlimited number of instances (limited only by the number of available agents).

Click on **VCS Settings** to move to the next step of creating a build configuration.

VCS roots and VCS settings

Next up is creating VCS roots for use in the build configuration. A VCS root is basically a collection of settings needed to use a particular repository in your build configurations and projects. VCS roots can be shared by build configurations in a project and across projects as well.

Click on the **Create and attach new VCS root** button to go to the VCS creation page. The first step is to choose the VCS type. The choices include **SVN**, **CVS**, **Perforce**, **Git**, and **Mercurial**, among others. As previously mentioned, we will be using Git as our VCS and the example project is hosted on GitHub. So, we will choose **Git** as the VCS type for this root, which loads further settings.

A typical VCS root configured for use with a Git repository on GitHub will have a configuration page similar to what is shown in the following screenshot:

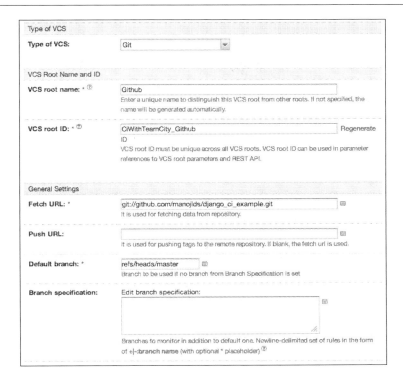

VCS root name and **VCS root ID** are again similar to the settings we saw for build configurations and projects.

For the Git repository, we will be using the **Fetch URL** option under the **General Settings** section. Here, we have configured it to use the `git://` URL provided by GitHub. We can also use the `ssh` URL or the `https` URL. Note that **Fetch URL** can be any remote URL in the formats accepted by Git.

> For most build configurations that only need to fetch the source from the repository, the `git://` URL is ideal as it is meant for such read-only use cases. In scenarios where there is a need to have a repository that is to be updated, for labeling, pushing commits, deploying to Heroku and others, we may have to use a `ssh` URL or a `https` URL.

All other settings are left to their defaults, but we will go through them to see how they are of use. The **Push URL** setting is used to specify the URL through which we can push tags from the steps run in the build configuration. It is of use if we have to use a separate fetch URL for checking out and a separate push URL to which we can push tags. Leaving this setting empty will make use of the fetch URL for such push purposes too.

The **Default branch** is the branch that is to be checked and also monitored for changes. By default, it will be `refs/heads/master`, that is, the `master` branch.

> The `master` branch is the default branch that is automatically created when we create a new Git repository. It is similar to the trunk branch that is created in VCSs such as SVN.

When we are building release builds out of a branch, we can use that specific branch in this setting, say `refs/heads/master/1.1.0`. The **Branch specification** setting allows us to define additional branches/refs that need to be monitored for changes. **Use tags as branches** allows tags to be treated as branches in the **Branch specification** settings.

Username style defines how a user on TeamCity can link their username to authors of commits in the VCS. The default is **Userid**, which is ideal.

The **Submodules** settings define whether submodules must be checked while cloning/updating the repository. The default, and recommended, setting is to use **Checkout**, which means submodules are checked out and updated when the parent repository is cloned and updated. The other option is to ignore submodules.

> Submodules are subrepositories contained within a parent Git repository. Submodules enable one repository to live within another as a subfolder but still be treated as a separate repository of its own. Consider the example of **Build and Release** scripts. They are common to many projects, and it is ideal to have them collocated with each project that needs them. Without duplicating such scripts, the **Build and Release** scripts can be maintained as a separate repository and added as submodules to the project repository that needs it.

The **Authentication** settings are used to, as the name suggests, specify the different ways to authenticate against the repository URL to fetch and push sources. The different options are as follows:

* The default is **Anonymous**, which works out for us, since we are using the `git://` URL for an open source application on GitHub.

- The **Default Private Key** option is used for ssh URLs and is similar to how ssh behaves by default. It will use the configurations present at <TeamCity user home>/.ssh/config, or if the configurations are not present, the private key at <TeamCity user home>/.ssh/id_rsa is used for authentication.

- The **Private Key** setting allows us to define a specific private key to be used instead of the configured default.

- The **Password** authentication method uses standard usernames and passwords for authentication.

Server settings specific to Git include conversion of line endings while doing checkout. If line endings are to be converted to CRLF on checkout, this setting needs to be enabled. A custom clone directory on the server is used to specify the path on the server where the repository is to be cloned. This can be left blank to use the default location.

Agent settings apply to using Git on the agent. The path to Git specifies the path of the Git binary explicitly. If left blank, TeamCity will look for the Git binary in few default locations, including the locations specified in the PATH environment variable. The **Clean policy** is used to define when the sources are to be cleaned using the git clean command, with every run of the build configuration, change of branch specified, or never. The decision to use this option depends on the kind of build process we are using and other factors. Cleaning will remove time savings provided by incremental builds. For our current purposes, we will leave it as the default setting of cleaning only on branch changes.

Checking Interval defines how frequently TeamCity has to poll the repository URL for changes. It can be left as the default of 60 seconds. To reduce the load on repository servers, we may consider making it higher, say 300 seconds or more.

We can click on the **Test Connection** button to see whether the configuration is okay. With a **Connection Successful** remark, we can save the VCS root and attach it to the build configuration.

 If the connection test is not successful, make sure that the repository URL and the authentication settings are fine. Depending on how we want to use the VCS root, the tools needed for the VCS may have to be installed on the server as well as all the agents.

Once the VCS root is added and attached, we can tune the VCS settings to be specific to the build configuration. The **Checkout** settings set set whether if checking out has to be done on the server and copied over as files and directories to the agent, or whether the checkout has to happen on the agent. The third option is not to check out any sources, in which case, no additional sources are needed apart from the scripts specified in the build configuration.

> Using the **Server-side** or **Agent-side** checkout is highly dependent on the specific scenario. The server-side checkout performs a Git clone on the server to get the source code and copies them over to the agent for build purposes. The build scripts running on the agent cannot make use of any repository-related activities. This is the ideal setup for most build configurations. It is also easier to configure, as now, only the server needs to have the VCS tools installed. The **Agent-side** checkout performs the actual clone on the agent. This might be needed in scenarios where the build involves using repository commands, such as doing `git push` to a server.

Clean all files before build specifies whether all the sources have to be cleaned (on the server or agent, as configured) and re-cloned before performing the build. This is generally not needed, and if used, will increase the load on the repository server, and the running time of the builds, as `git clone` generally takes long for even medium-sized repositories.

VCS labeling is about tagging the commits with information about the particular build that they were part of. We can tag successful builds or all builds irrespective of success or failure. In our setup, we will choose not to tag each and every build (even if just the successful ones) The final setting, **Display options**, describes whether the build configuration page should show changes from submodules as well, along with the repository changes.

Having configured the VCS for the build configuration, we can move on to adding the build steps for it, and actually make it do something.

Introducing the build steps

Build steps are the individual sequential tasks that are performed within a build configuration. Each build step is defined by a runner, which is a collection of predefined settings to use a particular tool such as Rake, Powershell, or even the plain command line. TeamCity comes with a number of build runners targeted at different platforms and build tools to ease the process of setting up build steps. There are plugins available to add even more build runners depending on the project's needs.

The most flexible of these is the **Command Line** build runner, which basically allows us to run a simple command or script directly in the command line. Even though there is a plugin available (which provides a Python runner), to keep things simple at the moment, we will use the **Command Line** runner.

 Most of the time, it is ideal to have the steps for our builds in a script, say `build.sh`. Running our builds should generally involve running the said script with minimal parameters. Here, we are using the actual commands for simplicity.

For the `build` build configuration, we will be adding two build steps. First we will perform code error, style, and complexity checking using the `flake8` tool. The command to be used is:

```
flake8 --exclude=migrations --ignore=E501,E225,E128,E126 .
```

Next, we will run the unit tests of the project, using the following command:

```
python manage.py test
```

We will choose the **Command Line** runner as the **Runner type** for the build configuration. This loads the necessary settings, which can be configured as shown in the following screenshot:

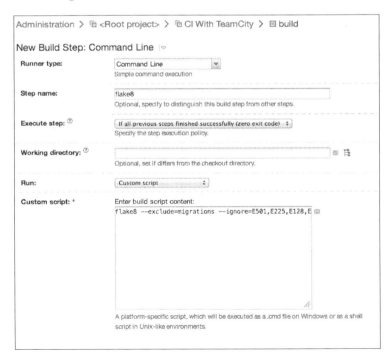

A **Step name** is used to give a descriptive name to the build step, which can help in easily identifying the build step when editing the build configuration at a later point in time and while perusing the log of the build configuration. We name it `flake8`.

Execute step specifies the condition that must be satisfied before the build step can run. The various options and their effects are described as follows:

- **If all previous steps finished successfully (zero exit code)**: The build step is run only if all the previous steps for the build configuration that have run on the agent have passed. This is the most common option, as generally, we want to proceed only if all the previous build steps were successful.

- **Only if build status is successful**: The builds step is run only if all the status of the build configuration is deemed successful as obtained from the server. Build status is not necessarily dependent on build step success as a build status may be set to failed by a failing test.

- **Even if some of previous steps failed**: The build step is run even if some of the previous steps might have failed. For example, this is useful for generating reports that give more information on previous failures.

- **Always, even if build stop command was issued**: The build step is run even if the build configuration is cancelled midway. This is useful for doing some cleanup before stopping the build.

We will use the default **If all previous steps finished successfully (zero exit code)** option in this case, even though this is the first build step.

Working directory for the command/script to be run as part of the runner can be changed if needed. If left blank, it will be the root of the checkout directory.

The **Run** setting allows us to either run the build step as a command with its associated parameters separately or run it as a script. The former works for simple commands and the latter is for complicated commands or to run multiple commands. We will run the `flake8` command through a script in this instance.

With all the necessary settings provided, we can **Save** the build step and add it to the build configuration. This is the point that the build configuration is actually created and available to be scheduled.

We will continue and add the next step, which will run the unit tests for the application. Additional steps can be added from the resulting page by clicking on the **Add build step** button. The rest of the steps are similar to the ones for the previous build step and only the actual command differs.

 Build steps are run in the sequence they are defined in the configuration. We can easily change the order of already-defined build steps by clicking on the **Reorder build steps** button on the build steps configuration page. In the resulting dialog, we can move the build steps to the desired position in the sequence.

Running our first build

We can go back to the **TeamCity Overview** page. We should now be able to see our newly created project, **CI With TeamCity**, and the newly created build configuration, `build`, within it.

We can click on the **Run** button next to the build configuration to immediately run it. The build configuration should run and report a success message. We can look at the log of the build configuration by hovering the mouse over the down arrow next to the status message and clicking on **Build log**. The build, and our CI, is very basic at the moment, but that will change pretty soon!

 The ellipsis (...) near the **Run** button can be used to trigger custom builds. From the pop up that appears on clicking this build, we can specify the agent to run this build and the VCS changes to include and also change the parameters defined for this build as needed.

Let's do some more editing with our build configuration. We can go back to the build configuration edit page by going to the **Administration** page by clicking on the link in the navigation bar and then navigating to the build configuration in question. Alternatively, from the overview page, we can go to the build configuration detail page and click on the **Edit Configuration Settings** link to get there directly.

On the right-hand side bar in the settings page, we can see eight settings sections. We covered the first three—**General Settings**, **Version Control Settings**, and **Build Steps**—while creating the build configuration. We will address the next two, **Build Failure Condition** and **Build Triggers** in the next two sections and others further on in this chapter.

Build failure conditions

This page provides settings for when the build configuration fails. The following screenshot shows how this page is configured by default:

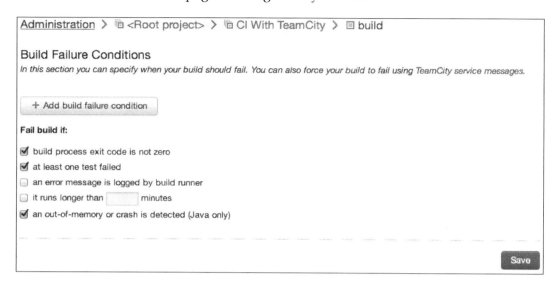

There are five basic build failure conditions:

- **build process exit code is not zero**: When enabled, it will fail the build if any of the steps exited with a non-zero error code

- **at least one test failed**: When enabled, it will fail the build even if one test failed

- **an error message is logged by build runner**: When enabled, it will fail the build if a build runner (in a build step) of the build configuration reports an error message (irrespective of the exit code)

- **it runs longer than x minutes**: When enabled, it will fail the build if it runs longer than the configured *x* minutes

 We recommended you set this condition as it ensures that a hanging build is cleared. This ensures that our other builds are not starved of agents stuck in hanging builds. Apart from hanging builds, this condition is also useful to ensure that builds don't keep getting longer over time.

- **an out-of-memory or crash is detected**: When enabled, it will fail the build if the JVM crashes or runs out of memory (and hence only applicable to Java based builds)

We will leave the defaults as is, though the JVM-based failure condition can be unchecked in the case of our sample project.

Apart from these basic build failure conditions, there are two other more advanced build failure conditions that are accessed by clicking on the **Add build failure condition** button:

- **Fail build on metric change**: This failure condition can be used to fail the build if it fails to satisfy certain metrics, such as artifact size, time taken to run the tests, coverage, and others. Also, the metric can be compared with previous successful builds, last pinned builds, or even a specific build in the past.
- **Fail build on specific text in build log**: This failure condition is to fail the build if the build log contains a specific text, say **failed to connect to database**. This is highly useful in cases where we use the command-line runner and the command doesn't return a proper exit code on failure.

We will not be adding any of these more advanced failure conditions for our current build configuration.

Triggering the build on VCS changes

Our build configuration doesn't have any **Build Triggers** associated with it. This means that it can only run if triggered manually, just as we did once already. The **Build Triggers** section defines various scenarios that can cause the build to be run automatically.

The three most common build triggers are:

- **VCS trigger**: This build trigger will poll the VCS for changes and will add the build to the build queue if it detects any change
- **Schedule trigger**: This build trigger will add the build to the build queue as per a schedule, similar to a cron job
- **Finish build trigger**: This build trigger will add the build to the build queue after another specified build has finished

Retry build trigger is used if we want to retry a build on failure. **Branch Remote Run trigger** is used to trigger personal builds on changes to specific branches. The other triggers are build tool-specific triggers (Maven and NuGet).

TeamCity has the personal build feature that allows us to run the build for the changes that we have on our workstation but are yet to push to the main repository. These builds are run separately from the normal builds and are visible only to the user involved. This feature can be used to run our local builds directly on the server before pushing the changes.

For our build configuration, we will add a VCS trigger so that commits to the Git repository trigger builds automatically. A typical VCS trigger configuration will be set up as shown in the following screenshot:

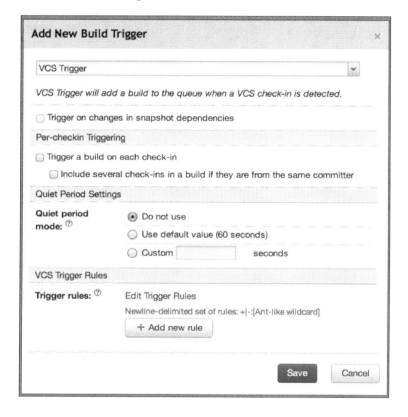

The **Trigger on changes in snapshot dependencies** option is used when triggering build chains, and we will be looking at such build chains later in the chapter. The other options in the VCS trigger configuration are explained as follows:

- **Per-checkin Triggering**: This controls whether the build configuration has to be triggered for every check-in that happens in the repository. It can be further tweaked to group several check-ins from one committer that came in sequentially to trigger only one build. This option is not generally required for CI as we are fine with triggering builds for a group of check-ins that came in within the time that TeamCity had polled the repository previously.

- **Quiet Period Settings**: This setting helps to specify the amount of time, if any, that TeamCity has to wait for the next VCS change in the repository before adding the build to the queue. We will leave it to the default value of not having any quiet periods, but this might be necessary in big projects with lots of check-ins happening at the same time, in order to relax the resource usage.

- **Trigger rules**: They specify the paths within the repository whose changes either do or don't cause the build to be triggered. For example, if there is a `Documentation` folder maintained in the source code, we may not want to trigger builds when the documentation is updated by someone. We can add something like `-:Documentation/**` as a trigger rule to prevent build triggering for changes in that folder.

We can save the trigger and from now on, any source code change in the repository will trigger our `build` build configuration.

Build chains

Our CI has only the `build` build configuration which looks for changes in the source code and runs a code style and error check and runs unit tests. In this section, we will look at adding build configurations to deploy our Django web application and also run some functional tests.

Deploying to Heroku

We will first add one more build configuration to deploy our web application to a testing environment. In our case, we will deploy our Django web application to Heroku.

Heroku is a cloud application platform with the ability to easily deploy and host web applications written using various languages and frameworks, including Rails and Django. The steps needed to make a Django application ready to be deployed to Heroku are given in detail at https://devcenter. heroku.com/articles/getting-started-with-django. Our sample project, django_ci_example, has already been equipped with the changes necessary to deploy it to Heroku.

We will start by adding a new build configuration with the name deploy-to-test. The steps to create the build configuration will be similar to the ones we took to create the build build configuration.

 Alternatively, we can go to the build configuration edit page for build, copy it, and create the new deploy-to-test build configuration.

The deploy-to-test build configuration will differ from the build in VCS settings. We will want to use the agent-side checkout mode for this build configuration as deploying to Heroku involves performing git push. The deploy-to-test build configuration will not have any build triggers at the moment. We will come back to triggers when we need to configure the build chain.

In the build steps, we will add a single command-line runner build step with the following commands:

```
git remote add heroku git@heroku.com:django-ci-example.git
git push heroku master
```

The build step adds a new Git remote pointing to the app's Git repository on Heroku and pushes to this newly created remote. It is to run the Git commands that we preferred agent-side checkout for this build configuration.

Let's manually run this build configuration too and see whether everything works as expected. Once the Heroku deploy is successful, the app should be accessible in Heroku. I have deployed the app at http://django-ci-example.herokuapp.com/ polls/.

Adding functional tests

Let's add a build configuration that will run Selenium functional tests against the deployed app.

 Selenium is a tool to automate web browsers. It is arguably the most popular tool used for functional test automation and has client libraries to write tests in most popular programming languages, including Java, C#, Python and Ruby. More details about Selenium can be found at `http://docs.seleniumhq.org/`

Our sample project already has a functional test, albeit a very basic one, using `Selenium WebDriver` added to it. The functional test can be run using the command:

```
python manage.py test polls.tests.FunctionalTests
```

The tests require the `DJANGO_APP_URL` environment variable to be set and pointing to the deployed version of the app. The tests while hit the app at this URL when they are running.

We will start by adding one more build configuration `functional-tests`, which is pretty much similar to the previous build configuration, except the command that is run in the build step is different.

As noted, we need to set an environment variable `DJANGO_APP_URL` so that the tests know where to find the deployed app. This is where one other section of build configuration settings comes into the picture—build parameters.

Parameters and build parameters

Parameters is the TeamCity concept to define and share settings across different entities, and to the build tools that actually run the builds. Parameters can be defined for a specific build configuration, project, agent or even a single run of a build. The parameters that are defined for a build configuration are known as build parameters.

 As previously mentioned, using the **Run custom build** option (… near the **Run** button), the predefined parameters for a build configuration can be changed for a particular run of the build configuration. TeamCity also provides special handling and validation for such parameters. For example, we can enter passwords (say, for a server to deploy to) in a password field rather than the usual text field while triggering the builds.

There are three types of build parameters that can be set on a build configuration:

- **Configuration Parameters**: These are limited to configurations within TeamCity. For example, we have been defining the build format for build configurations as `1.0.%build_counter%`. We can extract the `MAJOR.MINOR` version information as a **Configuration Parameter**, say `MAJOR_MINOR`, and use `%MAJOR_MINOR%%build_counter%` in the build format. Such parameters are of use when we start basing our build configurations off templates and also want to share such settings across projects.

- **System Parameters**: These are parameters that are passed to build tools, such as Ant and MsBuild, which use the property notation. These have special meaning for the build tool and are not supported by all the build tools.

- **Environment Parameters**: These are set in the build processes' environment as environment variables and can be accessed by the build tool and scripts by using the appropriate notation.

It is **Environment Parameters** that we will set and use in our `functional-tests` build configuration. We can head to the build parameters section on the build configurations edit page to add the required parameter. Clicking on the **Add new parameter** button brings up a dialog similar to the following screenshot:

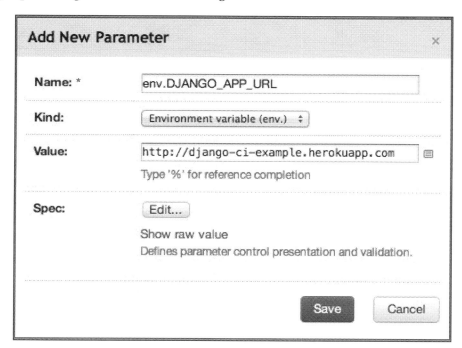

We name the parameter DJANGO_APP_URL and change the **Kind** to **Environment variable (env.)**. This updates the name to **env.DJANGO_APP_URL**. We provide the URL of the deployed app on Heroku as **Value** for this parameter.

The **Spec** setting is used to define how the parameter is to be presented in the **Run Custom Builds** dialog.

Click on **Save** to add the environment variable as a parameter. This should now be automatically seen by our functional tests as an environment variable.

Let's trigger the functional tests manually to see whether things work before proceeding.

The functional-tests build configuration here was set to run the Selenium-based tests with the assumption that a display is available to the user used to run the agent. This is not the case in most CI setups as the agents will be running in headless mode.

One strategy is to use a virtual display server, such as **X virtual frame buffer** (**Xvfb**). Xvfb makes it possible for agents that do not have a display to run apps that do require an X server to function correctly.

Usually, the Xvfb server is started before the functional test is run. The functional tests are configured to use the virtual display (through the use of the DISPLAY environment variable.) Once the tests are run, the server is stopped.

There are also alternatives such as PyVirtualDisplay (https://pypi.python.org/pypi/PyVirtualDisplay). The Python package which makes it much easier to run Selenium tests through Xvfb. In the Ruby world, there is headless (https://github.com/leonid-shevtsov/headless) gem, which functions similarly.

Things are a bit different in the Windows world, obviously. It may be required to enable the **Allow the service to interact with desktop** option for the TeamCity agent service when using **Local System** account. Another strategy is not to use the service and just run the batch scripts to start and stop the agents. The Windows display can be kept active using a VNC server such as **UltraVNC**.

Depending on the platform and setup, a strategy mentioned here could be utilized to run functional tests in agents that are not connected to a display.

Setting up the build chain

We have our three build configurations—`build`, `deploy-to-test`, and `functional-tests`—in place. Currently, `build` gets triggered when VCS changes are triggered. The other two don't have any triggers and can only be triggered manually.

We want them to form a build chain or pipeline whereby new check-in triggers `build`, which then trigger `deploy-to-tests`, and which in turn, triggers `functional-tests`.

We will do this by making use of the **Dependencies** settings provided by TeamCity. In particular, we will be using the **Snapshot** dependencies feature to set up our build chain.

Snapshot dependencies

Currently, our three build configurations are not linked except for the fact that they use the same repository. Ideally, we would want every commit (or set of commits), to go through these three build configurations sequentially. Thus, if a set of commits A, B, and C, passed `build`, we would want that same set to pass `deploy-to-test` and `functional-tests` for us to deem that these commits have been successfully integrated into the mainline. We cannot be sure whether A is a good commit if only B and C were deployed to the test environment, even though A, B, and C were used in the build. Ensuring that dependent build configurations all take the same set of commits and run is the job of **Snapshot** dependency.

Let's click on the **Dependencies** link in the right-hand side bar of the build configuration settings page for `deploy-to-test`. Click on the **Add new snapshot dependency** button to bring up the following dialog:

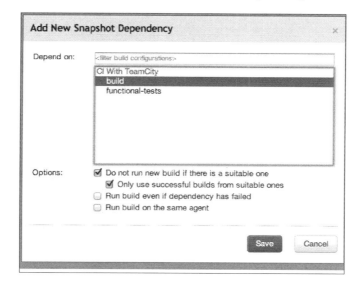

We will choose the `deploy-to-tests` build configuration to depend on the `build` build configuration. The options are explained as follows:

- **Do not run new build if there is a suitable one**: If there is a run of `build` that had the same source check-in as the ones we are trying to run for `deploy-to-tests`, then that build is seen as a suitable build and the `build` build configuration is not run again. **Only use successful build from suitable ones** limits it to successful builds only, rather than including failed ones as well.

- **Run build even if dependency has failed**: If it is enabled, when `build` is run due to the absence of a suitable build for `deploy-to-tests`, even if `build` fails, `deploy-to-tests` will still be triggered.

- **Run build on the same agent**: This is straightforward. It makes `build` and `deploy-to-tests` run on the same agent.

We will configure these options as shown in the previous screenshot. Click on **Save** to add the build dependency.

Similarly, we can add a **Snapshot** dependency to `deploy-to-test` from the `functional-tests` build configuration.

When we trigger (manually) `functional-tests`, the previous build configurations, `build` and `deploy-to-tests`, are run before running the `functional-tests`. But triggering build (through VCS changes or manually) doesn't run the other two dependent build configurations, which is what we want as well.

The Finish build trigger

To ensure that `build` triggers `deploy-to-test` and that `deploy-to-test` triggers `function-tests` successfully, we will make use of **Finish build trigger**, which we mentioned previously.

We will add a new build trigger to `deploy-to-test` and choose `build` as the build configuration. We will also make it trigger only on successful builds, as shown in the following screenshot:

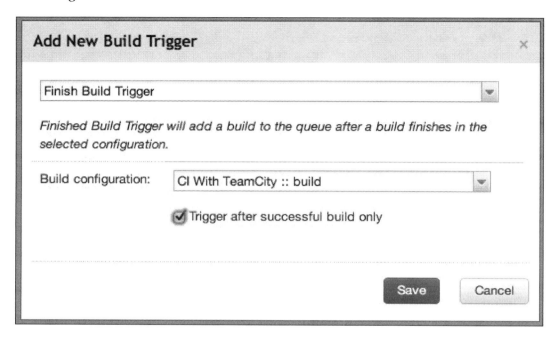

We will do the same with `functional-tests` and add `deploy-to-tests` as the build configuration to watch out for.

Next, we will remove the **VCS trigger** from `build` and move it to the final build configuration (also called root) of our build chain `functional-tests`. In our setup, all the build configurations have the same VCS root, and hence just triggering the root configuration on VCS change will ensure that the previous configurations in the chain are triggered as well due to the nature of **Snapshot** dependencies.

That's it! Our build chain has been set up and should start running our check-in through all three build configurations.

The Build chain view

The build chain view shows a visual representation of the build chain that we just configured. This view can be accessed from the project detail page or from the detail page of any build configuration that is part of the build chain. The following screenshot shows the build chain view:

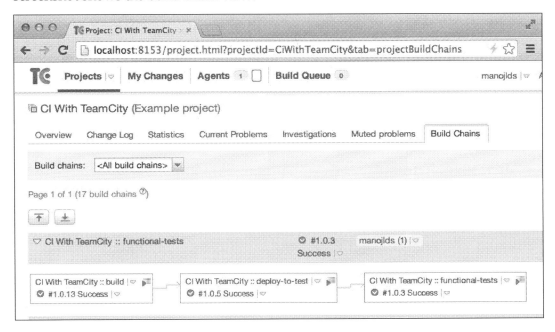

From this view, we can get information on each run of the build chain, with the latest at the top. We can also retrigger the build configurations to repeat the builds that happened in each chain.

With the completion of our build chain, our CI has got some real shape and is pretty functional. We will not stop here and will fine-tune it a bit more in the next section.

Fine-tuning our setup

Our CI setup is done, but as can be expected, it is a simple setup. While the aim of the chapter, and the book, is to highlight the TeamCity concepts involved in setting up CI, a real-world CI setup will not start off with everything in place from day one. Your CI setup may look very different a year from now than what it does today. In the coming section, we will be fine-tuning our setup to include coverage and test reports, and start using one of the most important features of TeamCity—artifacts.

Adding coverage and unit test reports

So far, we have been just running the unit tests as part of our build. Any developer or other member of the team who wants to know how many tests ran and in the event of failures, wants to know how many failed will have to go through the build logs to figure it out.

One of the main aims of CI (and hence, a CI tool) is to provide important information on the state of our builds as quickly as possible. TeamCity has many features that aid such quick information dissemination. One such feature is obtained through *unit test reports* and *status messages*. In the process of adding these reports, we will also start doing coverage analysis. Such metrics are an important part of CI.

We will start by changing the command we use to run the tests in `build` to the following:

```
python manage.py test polls --with-coverage --cover-package=polls
--cover-html --with-xunit
```

The additional arguments we have added are pretty self-explanatory. The `--with-xunit` flag makes our test runner create an XML report, which is in the same format as other unit testing frameworks, such as JUnit and Nunit. Reports in such formats are understood out of the box by TeamCity, and hence TeamCity can parse them and provide us with better information on the state of our builds.

Publishing reports as artifacts

Our test runner saves the coverage reports in the `cover` folder. Also, the `xunit` report that we wanted gets generated with the name `nosetests.xml`. Both of these items are created in the root folder of our project.

Once we have updated the command, let's go to the **General Settings** page of our `build` build configuration and update the **Artifact paths** to:

```
cover => coverage
nosetests.xml
```

The preceding setting will publish the cover folder as the coverage folder to the TeamCity server, which will expose it to us as an artifact that can be accessed from the web UI. The same happens with `nosetests.xml`.

XML report processing

Now, we will put `nosetests.xml` to better use. Let's go to the **Build Steps** section of the `build` build configuration's settings. This page provides the ability to add additional build features. Click on the **Add build feature** button and choose **XML report processing** in the resulting dialog. In the dialog, we can choose **Report type** as **Ant JUnit** and **Monitoring Rules** as `nosetests.xml`. We can optionally enable the **Verbose output** option, which provides more information in the logs when TeamCity finds and processes reports. A view of this dialog while setting this configuration is shown in the following screenshot:

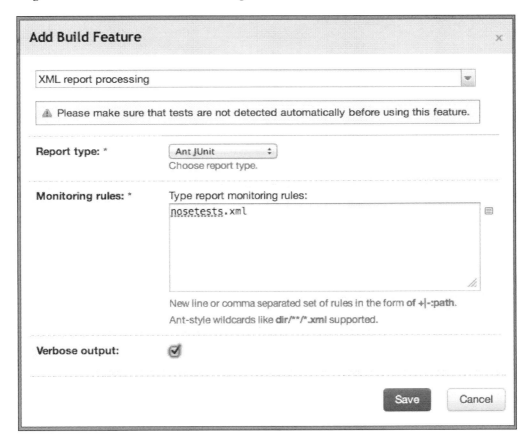

Click on **Save** to add this build feature.

We will head back to the projects page and trigger a manual run of `build` to see the results of our actions.

The following screenshot shows a view of the **Projects** page after the builds run successfully:

We can see that the status message is updated to **Test passed: 10, ignored: 1** instead of the dull and boring **Success** for `build`. Clearly, this gives us more rich information on what is happening in the build. In the case of test failures, we can easily see whether tests are failing, and if so, how many of them are failing.

Status messages can be updated directly from the build tools by emitting text in a certain syntax to the build log from the build tool. Such texts are called **service messages** and are especially useful when we use build tools that do not have out-of-the-box integration with TeamCity.

We also see that the coverage reports and the test report are available as artifacts for us to download, view, and even make use of in other build configurations if needed.

The advantages of XML report processing do not end here. We can also peruse the passed, failed, and ignored tests along with other statistics such as test duration from the **Tests** tab of the build run. This can be accessed by clicking on the test status message and clicking on the **Tests** tab, or by hovering the mouse over the down arrow next to the message to get the **Build Shortcuts** panel and clicking on the **Tests** link within it.

Report tabs

Rather than just having the coverage reports as artifacts only, we can make them more prominent by adding dedicated tabs for them in the TeamCity UI. Such **Report tabs** can be added to a build, as well as a project. Let's create a project report tab in this instance.

From the project settings page, click on the **Report Tabs** tab. Next, click on the **Create New Report tab** button. We can provide the **Tab Title** as `Coverage`. Choose the `build` build configuration for **the Get artifacts from** setting. Set up `coverage/index.html` as the **Start page**. Click on **Save** to add this report tab to the project.

We can now access the newly created tab from the details page of our project. The tab will contain the coverage output as shown in the following screenshot:

Build and project statistics

TeamCity provides statistics and graphs on various metrics involved with the build configurations and projects.

We can look at the **Statistics** tab of our `build` build configuration to get an idea of how such statistics are displayed. Important metrics such as build success rate, duration, and test count are shown as simple graphs.

It is also possible to add our own charts based on some prebuilt statistics maintained by TeamCity or even by values reported by various build tools.

Shared resources

We will fine-tune our CI setup once more around handling shared resources, such as external app servers, database servers, and others. Often, the various build configurations will need access to such external resources. The external resources have limitations, such as the number of connections that they can take, or the CI setup itself may dictate how shared resources may be accessed. In our current CI setup, we deploy the application to Heroku and run the functional tests against this deployed version. We do not want newer check-ins to start another deployment to Heroku while we are running the functional tests.

The Heroku instance of the app is a shared resource between our `deploy-to-test` and `functional-tests` build configurations. In our simple TeamCity installation, we have only one agent, and it will be the case that any newly scheduled `deploy-to-test` builds can only happen after the previous run's functional tests have finished. In a typical TeamCity installation, there will be more than one agent, if not tens of them, and such shared resources have to be handled appropriately.

Thankfully, TeamCity comes with a simple way to handle such shared resources. TeamCity's shared resource handling is based on the concept of *read and write locks*. In our deployment and test example, deployment is a `write` activity to the resource, and `functional-test` is a `read` activity (more complex tests perform writes too).

Build configurations obtain read and/or write locks on the resource as they start running. Other build configurations, will request such locks when they are ready to run. When a running build configuration has a read lock on a resource, other build configurations can obtain read locks on that resource too and start running. Build configurations that need write locks cannot start running if there are already build configurations running with read locks or write locks on the same resource.

Resources are classified into three types as follows:

- **Infinite Resource**: Such a resource can have an unlimited number of read locks on it.
- **Resource with quota**: There is a limit specified on the number of read locks that can be obtained on such a resource.
- **Resource with custom value**: The resource has various values, each of which can have locks on it. Some build configurations may lock all the values; some will be fine with any available value, and some need specific values.

To add a resource denoting the Heroku instance, from the configuration page for our project, click on the **Shared Resources** tab. Click on **Add new resource**, and in the resulting dialog, enter `heroku_app` as **Resource Name**. In our case, we will set **Infinite Resource** as **Resource Type**. Once we have added the shared resource to our project, we can add the corresponding locks to the build configurations involved.

Let's head to the **Build Steps** settings page for our `deploy-to-test` build configuration. Let's add a new build feature by clicking on the **Add build feature** button, and choose **Shared Resources** as the build feature. Now, we need to add a write lock on our `heroku_app` lock.

Click on the **Add lock** button and choose **heroku_app** as the resource involved. Specify **Write Lock** as the **Lock Type** on this resource and click on **Save** to add this lock. The resulting dialog after the lock is added is shown in the following screenshot:

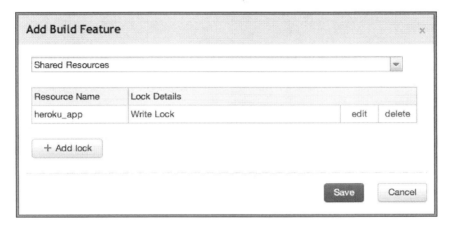

Click on **Save** to add the build feature to the build.

We will repeat the steps and add the **Shared Resources** build feature for the functional tests build configuration too. Only, in this case, it will be **Read Lock**.

In our setup, it doesn't matter whether the functional tests get a read lock or a write lock as, if the deploy is running, the functional tests can't run and vice versa. But in more complex cases, if for example, multiple build configurations are added to run functional tests in a parallel way to reduce the build times, it is necessary that all these build configurations have **Read Lock** on the resource so that they can all run at the same time.

With the shared resource setup done, we have ensured that we do not inadvertently trigger deployments when the functional tests are still running.

Agent Requirements

The **Agent Requirements** page specifies which agent(s) can possibly run a build configuration. Based on the OS of the agent, the various tools installed on it that may be needed for a build, and other factors, we may have cases where only certain agents can run certain build configurations.

One very common example of this with respect to web application development is around multiple browser testing. We want to test our app against various browsers and that too in multiple operating systems. Hence, we will create build configurations such as `functional-tests-chrome-ubuntu`, `functional-tests-chrome-windows`, and so on. For build configurations like these, we need to specify the requirements that the build configuration needs from the agent.

In our setup, let's think of a case where we need an agent that has Firefox installed to run our `functional-tests` build configuration. We can provide this requirement from the **Agent Requirements** settings page. Click on the **Add New Requirement** button.

In the resulting dialog, we will add a parameter called `firefox.installed` and set a requirement that the value equals true. Click on **Save** to add this requirement.

The page updates to show that there are no compatible agents for this build configuration as we are yet to say that this agent does indeed have Firefox installed on it. The current state of the **Agent Requirements** page for this configuration can be seen from the following screenshot:

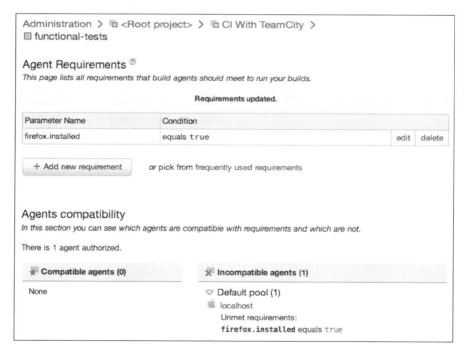

Next, we need to add the `%firefox.installed%` parameter to the agent to indicate that the agent satisfies this requirement. This is done by editing the agent's `buildAgent.properties` file located at `<TeamCity Agent Home>/conf`. At the end of this file, we will add the following line of code:

```
firefox.installed=true
```

The agent has to be restarted for this new parameter to be picked up.

Once this is done, we will see that the agent is added back as a compatible agent for our `functional-tests` build configuration.

 Just as we can see compatible agents for a build configuration, we can also see compatible build configurations for an agent by navigating to the particular agent's detail page (using the **Agents** link on the navigation bar) and visiting the **Compatible Configurations** tab.

With this, we have covered the important TeamCity concepts and features involved in setting up a simple but functional CI for our project.

Summary

In this chapter, we went through the TeamCity concepts involved in setting up CI for a sample project. Many of the basic as well as advanced TeamCity concepts and features were discussed. The steps in configuring a functional CI setup, from TeamCity's point of view, can be summarized as follows:

- Create the necessary projects
- Add the appropriate build configurations to the projects
- Configure dependencies across build configurations
- Set up triggers to run the builds based on various conditions
- Iterate as necessary to make improvements and tweaks

We will be discussing and using many more of the features that TeamCity has to offer in the upcoming chapters.

4
TeamCity for Java Projects

In this chapter, we will be looking at the specific features that TeamCity provides to set up CI for Java projects. We will be covering the following topics in the context of how they can be implemented using TeamCity:

- Using Ant build files to build a Java project
- Performing simple and complex Maven lifecycle activities for our project
- Getting started with building a project with Gradle
- Learning about database migrations, and their role in CI

In the process, we will be also be looking at other essential tools in the Java ecosystem, such as JUnit, Emma, JaCoCo, and more. We will also be exploring the rich integration that TeamCity has with these tools, thereby making it very simple and straightforward to set up our builds.

Using Ant with TeamCity

Apache Ant (`http://ant.apache.org/`) is a build tool along the lines of Make, especially for Java projects. It is written in Java, and hence provides the ability for teams already using Java to extend their build tool using Java as well. However, Ant is not limited to Java projects alone and can be used to build any source code, including .NET, Python, and Ruby.

The build files in Ant are written using XML, and one of the main features of Ant is its cross-platform nature. We will first cover some basics of Ant, including installation, a sample build file, and getting Ant to build our Java source code in a developer workstation, before proceeding to set up Ant builds on TeamCity.

Installing Ant

Ant packages can be downloaded from `http://ant.apache.org/bindownload. cgi`. Installing Ant involves extracting the downloaded package and adding the bin directory to the PATH environment variable. Also, the ANT_HOME environment variable has to be set up, pointing to the extracted folder location:

```
wget http://www.trieuvan.com/apache/ant/binaries/apache-ant-1.9.3-bin.
tar.gz

tar xvfz apache-ant-1.9.3-bin.tar.gz

export ANT_HOME="~/Downloads/apache-ant-1.9.3"

export PATH="$PATH:$ANT_HOME/bin"
```

 Ant can also be installed using a package manager on your OS of choice. For example, on Ubuntu, Ant can be installed just by running `apt-get install ant`.

With the previous set of commands, first we download the binary distribution using the `wget` command. Then, we extract the just-downloaded file using the `tar` command. We then set the ANT_HOME environment variable to the location that we extracted Ant to. We also add the bin folder in ANT_HOME to PATH so that the Ant command is available for use.

 The steps given previously will change slightly for different operating systems. The essential steps are downloading the package, decompressing it, and adding environment variables.

The environment variables set using the `export` command are available only for the current session. To persist these environment variables, steps appropriate to the platform, such as adding these commands to the `~/.bash_profile` file, have to be performed.

Building with Ant build files

A simple Ant build file to build a Java source will look like the following code:

```
<project name="ant_ci_example" default="dist" basedir=".">
  <description>
    Build file for sample Java project
    </description>
    <property name="src" location="src"/>
    <property name="build" location="build"/>
```

```
    <property name="dist"  location="dist"/>

    <target name="init">
      <mkdir dir="${build}"/>
    </target>

    <target name="compile" depends="init">
      <javac srcdir="${src}" destdir="${build}"/>
    </target>

    <target name="dist" depends="compile">
      <mkdir dir="${dist}/lib"/>

      <jar jarfile="${dist}/lib/ant-ci-example.jar"
basedir="${build}"/>
    </target>

  <target name="clean">
    <delete dir="${build}"/>
    <delete dir="${dist}"/>
  </target>
</project>
```

This is a basic build file that defines a project named ant_ci_example. Within it, we define a few properties using the `<property />` tag to configure where source code is located, where the build output is to be placed, and finally, where the distribution file needs to be generated.

> **Integrated Development Environment (IDE)**, like IntelliJ IDEA (also from JetBrains), can automatically generate an Ant build file if needed for a project. An Ant build file can be generated from the **Build | Generate Ant build...** menu.

We then define targets to clean our builds, perform a compile, and generate the distribution.

> A target in Ant, defined using the `<target />` tag, is a series of steps that perform some activity during the build process. As mentioned previously, `clean` is one of the targets defined in the build file that performs two cleanup steps—delete the build folder and delete the distribution folder. Ant has powerful concepts around targets, whereby targets can depend on other targets such that any execution of a particular target will also execute its dependencies. Ant also knows if a particular target has already been executed as part of the current build and will not execute it again.

The previous build file can be saved as `build.xml` in the directory with our Java source. Now, running Ant from the command line will run the build—execute the targets—and hence generate the needed distributions.

 When we run Ant from a directory, Ant will look for a file named `build.xml` by default. If we want to specify a different build file, we can use the `buildfile` flag:
```
ant -buildfile ant_ci_example_build.xml
```

Note that, in the build file, the project has the `dist` target as default, and hence when we run the build file with Ant, the `dist` target is executed. But, since the `dist` target has a dependency on the `compile` target, which itself has a dependency on the `init` target, the `init` and `compile` targets are executed as well, in that order. A heartening **BUILD SUCCESSFUL** message should inform us that everything is working fine. We can also see which targets were executed and what they did in the build log.

 It is possible to specify one or more targets that Ant has to run. For example, `ant clean` will call the clean target alone. The `ant clean init` command will call both the `clean` and `init` targets, in that order.

Building with Ant in a build configuration

With the basics of Ant done, it is time to set up TeamCity to perform the builds for us. As in *Chapter 3, Getting Your CI Up and Running*, I have set up a sample project on GitHub, which has Java source with the basic Ant build file that we just discussed. The project is located at `https://github.com/manojlds/Ant_CI_Example`.

We will begin by adding a new project—JAVA CI with TeamCity—and add a new build configuration within it— named `ant_build`. The VCS root for this build will be Git-based, and points to the repository on GitHub. These steps are similar to the ones we covered in *Chapter 3, Getting Your CI Up and Running*.

When it comes to adding a build step, we will choose **Ant** as the build runner in this case. A view of the settings that are to be configured for this build runner is shown in the following screenshot:

The **Path to a build.xml file** option allows us to specify the build file name. It is prepopulated with `build.xml`, which is Ant's default build file name. Alternatively, we can choose the **Build file content** option and specify the build file content directly in TeamCity.

> It is not recommended to use the **Build file content** option. It is ideal to have the build file version controlled in VCS along with the rest of the source code. This ties in with one of the practices of CI—everything that is needed to build the project is put in VCS with the rest of the source code.

Working directory can be specified if we want Ant to be executed from a directory other than the checkout directory. Leaving it blank uses the checkout root as the working directory. The **Targets** option is used to specify the name of the targets that are to be run. This is very much similar to how we can specify targets from the command line—using a space-separated list of targets. Leaving this blank will call the default target, which is fine for our build file.

Ant home path is the location of Ant that we would like to use for the build. TeamCity comes bundled with its own version of Ant (1.8.2 for TeamCity 8.0) that it uses automatically if this setting is left blank. We can alternatively provide this path if we want to use our own version of Ant (older or newer, as needed).

The **Additional Ant command line parameters** setting can be used to pass additional flags to Ant, such as the flag to produce verbose build output.

The build runner also provides the ability to set Java parameters—**JDK home path**, which is taken from JAVA_HOME if not specified, and other **JVM command line parameters**, such as memory settings. The latter can be tweaked as needed, based on the performance of the build task.

There are parameters related to **Test** and **Coverage** available for the Ant build runner too. The **Run recently failed tests first** option runs tests that failed in the previous build first, before other tests, so that we can get quick feedback on whether the failing tests have passed in this build. The **Run new and modified tests first** option runs new tests, or tests that were changed from previous builds first, for similar reasons.

Code coverage-related parameters allow us to configure coverage tools, which we will look into in detail in the upcoming sections of this chapter.

Click on **Save** to add the build step and create the build configuration.

> At this point, we can add VCS trigger to the build so that it starts building for every commit (or set of commits). We can leave it as is to trigger it manually.

Let's trigger the build to see the Ant build passing.

Adding some unit tests

With the basic build passing, it's time to add some unit tests. The unit tests' target in the updated build file is as follows:

```
<target name="unit-tests" depends="compile">
  <junit printsummary="yes" haltonfailure="yes" showoutput="true"
fork="true" forkmode="once">
    <classpath>
      <pathelement location="lib/junit-4.11.jar"/>
      <pathelement location="lib/hamcrest-core-1.3.jar"/>
      <pathelement location="${build}"/>
      <pathelement location="${src}"/>
    </classpath>
```

```
        <formatter type="xml"/>

        <batchtest fork="yes" todir="${reports.tests}">
          <fileset dir="${src.tests}">
            <include name="**/*Test.class"/>
          </fileset>
        </batchtest>
      </junit>
  </target>
```

The `dist` target now depends on `unit-tests` (we don't want a distribution that hasn't passed our tests). `unit-tests` depends on `compile` as we need to compile the source code before running the tests.

 The full contents of the `build.xml` file can be obtained at `https://github.com/manojlds/Ant_CI_Example/blob/master/build.xml`.

Due to TeamCity's close integration with Ant, the status message should be updated with the number of tests passed/failed information when the build finishes running, as shown in the following screenshot:

Setting up code coverage

We saw that the Ant build runner had options to set up code coverage. Let's also enable that feature now that we have unit tests running in our build. Go to the `ant_build` build configuration's edit page and then to the edit page of the build step.

 Emma and IntelliJ IDEA are the coverage tools supported out of the box by TeamCity up to 8.0.x. From 8.1, JaCoCo is also added as an available tool.

Let's add Emma as a coverage tool for the step.

The **Coverage instrumentation parameters** field is used to send additional parameters, such as filters for classes, to be ignored from coverage (in this case, the Test classes).

 For coverage to work properly, the tests must be run by setting fork="true" in the junit task in Ant. Also, the source must be compiled using debug flags by passing debug="true" to the javac task.

Adding the coverage to our build brings in a lot of useful features. The coverage reports are automatically uploaded to the TeamCity server, and they are available through the **Code Coverage** tab, accessed from the build run page of the build configuration, as seen in the following screenshot:

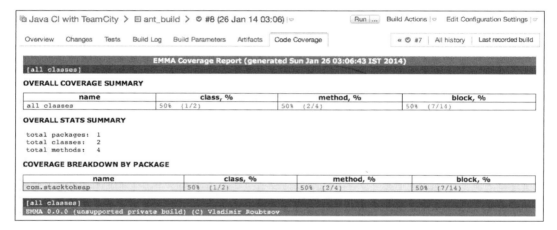

Additionally, the coverage trend can also be seen from the graphs available in the **Statistics** tab of both the build configuration and the project.

Build scripts versus TeamCity features

When adding coverage to our Ant build, we used the Emma coverage feature of the Ant build runner in TeamCity.

Alternatively, we could have used the Emma-based tasks available for Ant and have the coverage done from our build file itself.

This is a situation that is not specific to Ant alone. It can occur in any project/stack. A rule of thumb is that our build scripts should be able to do things the same way between the CI server and a local developer box. Using TeamCity features, such as the coverage in this case, obviously means that we won't be doing coverage the same way on a developer machine as well. While it is fine to use some features like the Ant build runner, which mainly provides an easy way to set up calls to Ant, it may not be OK to use other features, such as the Emma coverage provided by TeamCity.

Also, as mentioned, maintaining everything needed to build a project in VCS is an important CI principle. Having things like coverage configured in build scripts is the easiest way of being true to that principle. Relying on TeamCity to provide such features may not make that possible.

Having said all that, there are use cases where we may want to use the built-in feature, especially when we are starting out with CI as these features make it dead simple to set up the steps necessary for CI.

Also, since this book is about highlighting the various features that TeamCity brings to the table, the book will be going into detail about many of them, but it is not a recommendation to use these features in all scenarios.

System properties and Ant

We previously saw in *Chapter 3*, *Getting Your CI Up and Running*, that build parameters are classified into three types:

- Configuration parameters
- System properties
- Environment variables

We saw how configuration parameters and environment variables are used. System properties are very useful with tools like Ant. In our sample build file, we defined many properties, like the one to specify the path to the source build. Using system properties, it is possible to override these values, or even add new properties that can be used in our Ant build file. For example, our test reports were being created at the location specified by the `reports.tests` property:

```
<property name="reports.tests"  location="reports"/>
```

By adding a system property with the same name (but with a `system.` prefix) in TeamCity, we can automatically set this value to something else, say `teamcity-reports`. This step is shown in the following screenshot:

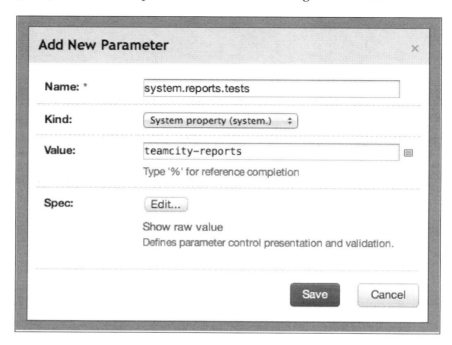

 These system properties are passed to the Ant command using the `-Dproperty-name=property-value` syntax. It is not only the user defined system properties, but the TeamCity generated ones, such as `build.vcs.number.1,` are passed to Ant as well.

Using the system properties in TeamCity is recommended over passing these ourselves through the command line. TeamCity properly escapes the properties when passing them to tools like Ant. Also, all the properties are defined in one page, so it is very easy to see what properties are needed and edit them when needed.

With the TeamCity features related to Ant covered, we will move on to the kind of support that TeamCity provides for another very popular Java tool—Maven.

Using Maven with TeamCity

Apache Maven (`http://maven.apache.org/`) is a build, deployment, and dependency management tool for Java-based projects. Maven really emphasizes convention over configuration. What this means is that it is very simple to start managing the build and deployment steps of our project with Maven by following simple conventions. We don't have to write a lot of custom tasks to get started, and therefore we can focus on the software itself, rather than spending a lot of time on how the software is built.

This can be contrasted with the Ant build file that we used in the previous section on Ant, even though that itself is a simple build file that doesn't do a lot of things. In the Ant build file, we had to use properties to specify the location of the source code, the directory where we wanted to generate the build output, and also the directory where we wanted to put the distribution. We then used these properties in various tasks, such as compiling and generating the JAR files. We also had to specify the classpath explicitly so that the `junit` task can find the necessary libraries for it to run.

In Maven, these locations are assumed to be located in certain directories. Source code, for example, is assumed to be located in `<root>/src/main/java`. The distributable is assumed to be generated at `<root>/target`, and so on. By following such conventions, Maven makes it very easy to get started with the builds. Also, it makes it very easy for people switching between projects, and also working on multiple projects, to know exactly what does what and what gets generated where.

 Convention over configuration means that there are some defaults that are assumed of the project. But project requirements change from team to team, and tools like Maven allow such customizations/ configurations to be done as well.

Assuming such defaults and having an opinionated framework like Maven works well for build and deployment purposes. These are tasks that vary little between projects. The usual activities of compile, running tests, and packaging, are almost the same, and they save minor differences. Yet, each team would end up writing their own build scripts that did virtually the same thing. Maven helps us in removing such duplication of work.

Enough with talking about Maven, let's start using it!

Installing Maven

Maven can be downloaded from `http://maven.apache.org/download.cgi`. The installation steps are pretty similar to what we saw for Ant:

```
cd /usr/local
wget http://mirror.symnds.com/software/Apache/maven/maven-3/3.1.1/
binaries/apache-maven-3.1.1-bin.tar.gz
tar xvfz apache-maven-3.1.1-bin.tar.gz
export M2_HOME=/usr/local/apache-maven-3.1.1
export M2=$M2_HOME/bin
export PATH=$M2:$PATH
mvn -version
```

> Maven can also be installed using a package manager on your OS of choice. For example, on OS X, if you are using `brew`, Maven can be installed using a command as simple as the following:
>
> `brew install maven.`

We change to the `/usr/local` folder and download the binary distribution from a mirror using `wget`. We extract the distribution using the `tar` command and set the necessary environment variables to get Maven working. We set the `M2_HOME` environment variable pointing to the directory we just extracted. The `M2` environment variable is set pointing to the bin directory within `M2_HOME`. To add the Maven command to path, we also add `M2` to `PATH`. Finally, we run `mvn --version` to verify that Maven is available and working fine.

> The installation procedures will vary between different operating systems, especially around setting the environment variables, including `PATH`. The export commands here affect these environment variables only in the current session.

Creating a Maven project

Maven comes with the `archetype` plugin, which can be used to generate our project following the standard Maven directory structure.

We can generate our project using the following command:

```
mvn archetype:generate -DgroupId=com.stacktoheap.maven_ci_example
-DartifactId=maven_ci_example -DarchetypeArtifactId=maven-archetype-
quickstart -DinteractiveMode=false
```

We run the Maven goal, provided by the archetype plugin, to generate a project. We use the `maven-archetype-quickstart` archetype to generate our project. There are various other archetypes available for us to choose from. The first time this command is run, it will take a while for Maven to complete as Maven will download all the dependencies and artifacts it needs.

When the command finishes, we will see a directory with the name `maven_ci_example`, which is the name we gave for `artifactId`. This directory has the structure followed by Maven projects. The source code is present at `maven_ci_example/src/main/java`, and `maven_ci_example/src/test/java` has the tests.

The `maven_ci_example` folder also has the `pom.xml` file.

Introducing the Project Object Model (POM)

The `pom.xml` file, named after Project Object Model, is the main configuration file used by Maven to build our project. The `pom.xml` file generated by the `archetype` plugin is as follows:

```xml
<project xmlns="http://maven.apache.org/POM/4.0.0" xmlns:xsi="http://
www.w3.org/2001/XMLSchema-instance"
   xsi:schemaLocation="http://maven.apache.org/POM/4.0.0 http://maven.
apache.org/maven-v4_0_0.xsd">
   <modelVersion>4.0.0</modelVersion>
   <groupId>com.stacktoheap.maven_ci_example</groupId>
   <artifactId>maven_ci_example</artifactId>
   <packaging>jar</packaging>
   <version>1.0-SNAPSHOT</version>
   <name>maven_ci_example</name>
   <url>http://maven.apache.org</url>
   <dependencies>
     <dependency>
       <groupId>junit</groupId>
       <artifactId>junit</artifactId>
       <version>3.8.1</version>
       <scope>test</scope>
     </dependency>
   </dependencies>
</project>
```

This defines a Maven project by the name `maven_ci_example`. The `<packaging>jar</packaging>` tag states that the project generates `jar` as the build output (a webapp would generate `war`, for example). The `pom.xml` also adds `junit` as a dependency, as a sample test class was also generated by the archetype plugin, under `maven_ci_example/test/java/com/stacktoheap/maven_ci_example/AppTest.java`.

We will not be going into the details of Maven in this book as that in itself is worthy of a book or two. We will touch on the necessary aspects of Maven needed to set up CI for a project using Maven in TeamCity. To understand more about Maven, I recommend the *Maven By Example* book by Tim O'Brien, John Casey, Brian Fox, Jason Van Zyl, Juven Xu, Thomas Locher, Dan Fabulich, Eric Redmond, and Bruce Snyder, found online at `http://books.sonatype.com/mvnex-book/reference/public-book.html`. If you are not using Maven already and are looking at starting to use Maven with TeamCity, I recommend a read of this book before proceeding.

Building the project

We can build our project using the `mvn install` command. This command will compile our project, run the `junit` tests, package it into JAR, and install it in the local Maven repository.

The `install` parameter to `mvn` can be seen as being similar to how we pass target names to the Ant command. These are called `goals` in Maven. When we used the `archetype:generate` command previously to generate our project, the `archetype:generate` was the goal. To be more specific, we are identifying the plugin, `archetype`, and the goal within that plugin, `generate`, to be executed.

Maven utilizes various plugins, such as `maven-jar-plugin` to generate the JAR file, and `maven-surefire-plugin` to run the unit tests. A section of the log, as generated by the previous command, is shown in the following screenshot:

```
Downloading: http://repo.maven.apache.org/maven2/org/apache/maven/surefire/surefire-junit3/2.12.4/surefire-junit3-2.12.4.jar
Downloaded: http://repo.maven.apache.org/maven2/org/apache/maven/surefire/surefire-junit3/2.12.4/surefire-junit3-2.12.4.jar (26 KB at 29.5 KB/sec)

-------------------------------------------------------
 T E S T S
-------------------------------------------------------
Running com.stacktoheap.maven_ci_example.AppTest
Tests run: 1, Failures: 0, Errors: 0, Skipped: 0, Time elapsed: 0.005 sec

Results :

Tests run: 1, Failures: 0, Errors: 0, Skipped: 0

[INFO]
[INFO] --- maven-jar-plugin:2.4:jar (default-jar) @ maven_ci_example ---
Downloading: http://repo.maven.apache.org/maven2/org/apache/maven/maven-archiver/2.5/maven-archiver-2.5.pom
Downloaded: http://repo.maven.apache.org/maven2/org/apache/maven/maven-archiver/2.5/maven-archiver-2.5.pom (5 KB at 6.6 KB/sec)
```

The previous screenshot shows how the `junit` tests are run by the Surefire plugin and then proceeds to generate the JAR file using `maven-jar-plugin`.

> Understanding the Maven build lifecycle is essential when working with Maven. As we build a project, the build process moves through various lifecycles and also phases within these lifecycles. Based on the plugins we use, and the configurations in our `pom.xml`, different goals get associated with different lifecycles and phases, and it is this association that gives the goals and the order in which they are executed.
>
> The `install` goal used in the `mvn install` command is tied to the install lifecycle phase. All the previous lifecycles phases are executed for a given goal/lifecycle, and this is the reason why the goals in previous phases, such as compile, test, and package, were executed as well.
>
> The `install` goal installs the generated JAR file into an appropriate location in the local Maven repository. In our case, it was installed to `~ /.m2/repository/com/stacktoheap/maven_ci_example/ maven_ci_example/1.0-SNAPSHOT/maven_ci_example-1.0- SNAPSHOT.jar`.

We have achieved a lot with a simple `pom.xml` file and didn't have to worry about adding `junit` to path, setting where the JAR file is to be generated, and so on. All of these were achieved by following the conventions set by Maven, and our project was following these conventions already because we used the `archetype` plugin to generate our project.

Using Maven in a build configuration

I have created a repository on GitHub for our project created in the previous section, which can be found at `https://github.com/manojlds/maven_ci_example`.

We will create a new build configuration with the name `maven_build` in our `Java CI with TeamCity` project. We will then create and attach a new VCS root pointing to the repository on GitHub. These steps are similar to the ones we covered in the previous chapter.

When it comes to adding a build step, we will choose **Maven** as the build runner. A section of the settings page for the build runner is given in the following screenshot:

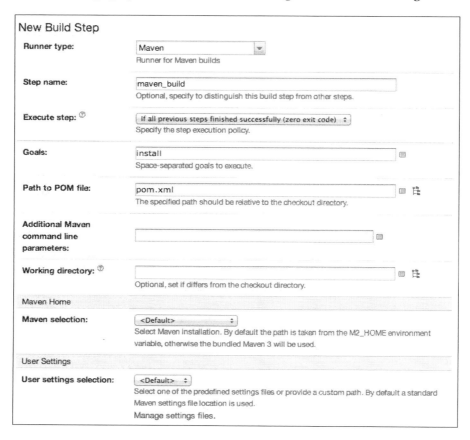

The **Goals** option is similar to the **Targets** options that we set for the Ant build runner. Here, we specify `install` as the goal that we want to run for our build configuration.

It is recommended to specify `clean install` as the goals so that we perform a cleanup before starting our builds. The clean goal will remove any directories and other output generated by previous builds. Clean and Install are different lifecycles, and therefore `mvn install` doesn't call the clean goal by default, and it needs to be called as `mvn clean install`.

The path to the POM file can be left at the default `pom.xml` value in our case but may be changed if we are using a POM file not located at the root.

Additional Maven command line parameters can be used to specify other parameters that we may want TeamCity to pass to the mvn command. One such parameter could be the -P flag used to set profiles.

 Maven build profiles provide the ability to specify environment-related information to a build. For instance, we can specify a profile dev for development purposes, and another one named ci to run on CI. They are usually specified in the pom.xml file or in a settings file.

The **Working directory** setting is used to define the working directory to execute the mvn command for the build.

The **Maven Home** section is used to define the location where Maven is installed on the agents running the build. The various options are explained as follows:

- The **<Default>** option will make TeamCity find a Maven installation pointed to by M2_HOME. If we want to use our own installation of Maven in TeamCity, we need to follow the previous installation instructions as the user under which the agent is running.

- The **<Custom>** option allows us to enter a path in the settings to the location where Maven is installed and removes dependence on the M2_HOME environment variable.

- The **Bundled Maven 2** and **Bundled Maven 3** options use the Maven versions (for 2.x and 3.x respectively) bundled with TeamCity. This is similar to using the bundled Ant.

We can choose the bundled Maven 3 in our case for simplicity, but it is recommended to maintain and use our own version of TeamCity so that developers can use the latest (or a specific version) Maven that is needed, rather than depending on the version that is bundled with TeamCity.

The **User Settings** section is used to specify the location of the Maven settings (settings.xml) file. This is usually located at ~/.m2/settings.xml. Using <Default> will use this path on the agent. By using <Custom>, we can specify a custom path to this file. We will leave it on <Default> in our case, as we don't depend on any settings from the file.

 Maven settings files are used to define servers, repositories, authentication, profiles, and other details.

Java parameters are similar to what we saw for Ant, used to specify the JDK path and also to provide any additional JVM parameters.

The **Use own local artifact repository** option can be checked to isolate the local repository of this particular build configuration from that of others.

The **Enable incremental building** option can be enabled to allow TeamCity to build only modules that are affected by the commits being used in the current build. TeamCity also has enough smarts to run only the tests that are affected. This option can be selected to reduce the build times. The ability to build incrementally is on top of such features provided by Maven itself.

We will not enable **Code Coverage** for our build configuration at this point in time.

Let's **Save** the build configuration and run it manually to see the fruits of our labor.

We should see our build configuration pass and also show the test information in the status message, as seen in the following screenshot:

We can also see from the screenshot that there is a link to the **Maven Build Info** tab, which gets added to build configurations using the Maven build runner. This tab provides information, such as the Maven projects in the build, the plugins used, and so on. The information provided is similar to the effective POM settings displayed by the `mvn help:effective-pom` command.

Setting version number

In our `pom.xml`, we have defined the version as:

```
<version>1.0-SNAPSHOT</version>
```

When we are building the project as part of the CI, we want to use a proper release version (which corresponds to the build number/version on TeamCity).

We can set a version on the `pom.xml` from the command line by running the following line of code:

```
mvn versions:set versions:commit -DnewVersion="1.0.1"
```

This will set the version to 1.0.1 during the build, and our `mvn` install will finally install the specified version in our repository.

We will perform this as a new build step for the `maven_build` configuration. Let's add a build step with Maven runner from the build configuration's settings page. The goals settings for this build step will be `versions:set versions:commit`. Save the build step to have it added to the build configuration. In the **Build Steps** page, we can click on **Reorder build steps** to move the new build step before the existing build step, which performs `mvn install`.

So how do we pass in `-DnewVersion="build number"` to the build step? If you thought system properties, you guessed it right!

We can head to the **Build Parameters** section and add a new **System property**. We provide the `%build.number%` parameter as the value for the `newVersion` system property. As we have seen previously, the `%build.number%` parameter has the build number of the current build.

This `newVersion` system property is automatically passed to Maven as `DnewVersion="build number"` while running the builds. Note that this is applied to both the build steps in the build configuration, but that is fine.

We can see the build number being appended to the names of the JAR files installed in our local repository when we perform `mvn install`.

Setting up code coverage for our build

We will be setting up code coverage for our build using the JaCoCo coverage runner along with its Maven plugin. We will begin by adding the following section to our `pom.xml` file:

```
<build>
  <plugins>
    <plugin>
      <groupId>org.jacoco</groupId>
      <artifactId>jacoco-maven-plugin</artifactId>
      <version>0.6.2.201302030002</version>
      <executions>
        <execution>
          <goals>
            <goal>prepare-agent</goal>
          </goals>
        </execution>
        <execution>
          <id>report</id>
```

```
        <phase>prepare-package</phase>
        <goals>
      <goal>report</goal>
        </goals>
      </execution>
    </executions>
  </plugin>
 </plugins>
</build>
```

We add the JaCoCo Maven plugin and hook it up in different execution phases so that it can run before the tests start running and also to ensure that JaCoCo coverage reports are generated in the end.

When we run `mvn install`, we can see that the JaCoCo reports are generated at `maven_ci_example/target/site/jacoco/index.html`.

Let's set up the reports as an artifact in our `maven_build` build configuration. Head to the configuration page for our `maven_build` build configuration. In **General settings**, under **Artifacts**, we can enter the following to package the reports located in the path into a `coverage.zip` file and expose it as an artifact on TeamCity:

```
target/site/jacoco/**/*.* => coverage.zip
```

We can trigger the build to see what happens. After the build passes, we can see that a shortcut link to **Code Coverage** is automatically added, as seen in the following screenshot:

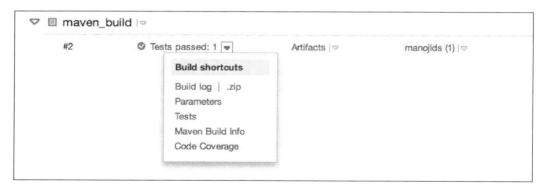

Clicking on this link takes us to the **Code Coverage** tab (added automatically), which shows the `index.html` page generated by JaCoCo.

How did this happen? TeamCity automatically recognizes artifacts named coverage.zip (and having an index.html file in the root) as coverage reports and sets up the **Code Coverage** tab for them. If we didn't follow this name, or just uploaded the artifact as a directory, we would have had to set up our own report tab pointing to the index.html file within the artifact.

 The ability of TeamCity to identify artifacts based on their names and automatically create tabs for them is configurable from the **Administration Page** | **Report Tabs** (under **Integrations** in the left-hand side bar.) In this page, we can see how the **Code Coverage** tab is created automatically on detecting coverage.zip as an artifact. We can edit this behavior or add new ones from this page.

The way we have set up coverage, using the JaCoCo plugin for Maven, does not provide statistics information regarding coverage. But even these are possible using a TeamCity feature called **service messages** (http://confluence.jetbrains.com/display/TCD8/Build+Script+Interaction+with+TeamCity), which we will explore in a future chapter. As of TeamCity 8.1, the JaCoCo coverage tool support is included out of the box. Using this, we get much tighter and easier integration with JaCoCo for our builds.

Maven on TeamCity, beyond the build runner

Support for Maven in TeamCity is not just limited to providing a build runner for it. In this section, we will be exploring some of the other Maven-related features that TeamCity provides, and which makes it a great CI tool for use with Maven.

Creating a Maven build configuration

So far, we have created build configurations for our Maven-based builds the usual way. You might have noticed from the settings page of a project that there is also a **Create Maven build configuration** button right next to the **Create build configuration** button. Clicking on this button takes us to the create settings page as seen in the following screenshot:

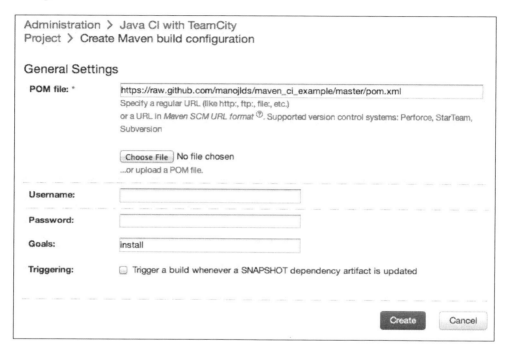

In this page, we can either enter the URL to the **POM file** for our Maven build or directly upload the POM file.

The pom.xml file should include scm settings for this to work. TeamCity needs this information to populate the VCS for the build configuration. The scm configuration for our sample project looks like the following snippet:

```
<scm>
<connection>scm:git:git://github.com/manojlds/maven_ci_example.git</
connection>
<developerConnection>scm:git:git://github.com/manojlds/maven_ci_
example.git</developerConnection>
<tag>HEAD</tag>
<url>https://github.com/manojlds/maven_ci_example</url>
</scm>
```

We can use `https://raw.github.com/manojlds/maven_ci_example/master/pom.xml` in our case.

The **Username** and **Password** provide the authentication settings needed to fetch the `pom.xml` file. **Goals**, as expected, configures the goals to run as part of the build. **Triggering** can be checked to trigger the build when a dependency of the project (as specified in the POM file) changes.

Clicking on **Create** creates the build configuration. TeamCity will use the settings from the specified `pom.xml` file to configure the build appropriately. This is a quick and easy way of creating our Maven build configurations.

 I recommend using the normal way of creating Maven build configurations. We can tweak all the important settings, such as the build options, and others, when we create our first build configuration and can then copy this build configuration to create new ones.

Global Maven settings file

From **Administration page** | **Maven settings** (found under **Integrations** in the left-hand side bar), we can upload a global settings file for use in the Maven builds.

As of TeamCity 8.1, it is now possible to specify the Maven settings for a project from the project's settings page. TeamCity uses these settings to get information about the repositories to trigger builds that use Maven-based triggers.

Setting up Maven-based triggers

TeamCity also comes with support to trigger dependent builds when their dependencies change in the repository. This support is over the artifact-based triggering mechanism.

There are two Maven-based triggers:

- **Maven Snapshot Dependency Trigger**: This triggers the build when any of the snapshot dependencies of the project change. The dependency information is obtained from the `pom.xml` file.

- **Maven Artifact Dependency Trigger**: This triggers the build when the dependencies of the project change. This includes both SNAPSHOT and version-based dependencies, unlike the Maven Snapshot Dependency Trigger, which only looks at SNAPSHOTS.

Do not confuse snapshot here with the Snapshot dependencies in TeamCity. The Snapshots concept mentioned here are Maven- specific.

We will look at the Maven Artifact Dependency Trigger in detail. I have created another sample project at `https://github.com/manojlds/maven_ci_dependant_example`. This project uses the `maven_ci_example` project as a dependency. The `pom.xml` file for both the projects are updated with the repository information to store and retrieve the artifacts from a remote repository. The addition to `pom.xml` for `maven_ci_example` is as follows:

```
<distributionManagement>
  <repository>
    <uniqueVersion>false</uniqueVersion>
    <id>maven_ci_repo</id>
    <name>Maven CI repo</name>
    <url>file:///Users/Admin/.m2/repository2</url>
    <layout>default</layout>
  </repository>
</distributionManagement>
```

When we run `mvn deploy`, Maven will deploy the JAR file and `pom.xml` of our project to the configured remote repository (which, for simplicity, is still a local filesystem location).

The `maven_ci_dependant_example` project has the `maven_ci_example` project as a dependency. It also configures the repository from which this dependency has to be fetched. The relevant sections of the `pom.xml` for this project are as follows:

```
<dependencies>
  <dependency>
    <groupId>com.stacktoheap.maven_ci_example</groupId>
    <artifactId>maven_ci_example</artifactId>
    <version>${maven_ci_example.version}</version>
  </dependency>

</dependencies>
<repositories>
  <repository>
    <id>maven_ci_repo</id>
    <url>file:///Users/Admin/.m2/repository2</url>
    <snapshots>
      <enabled>true</enabled>
    </snapshots>
```

```
        <releases>
          <enabled>true</enabled>
        </releases>
      </repository>
    </repositories>
```

With the `pom.xml` files set up, we can set up the triggers. We will add a new build configuration for the `maven_ci_dependant_example` project. We can do this by simply copying the `maven_build` build configuration and then changing the VCS root and other settings as needed. We can call this `maven_dependant_build`. We will also update the build step of the `maven_build` to do `mvn deploy`, rather than `mvn install`, so that we can deploy the project to the configured remote repository.

Heading to the **Build triggers** section of the `maven_dependant_build` build configuration, we can add the **Maven Artifact Dependency Trigger**. The necessary configuration is seen in the following screenshot:

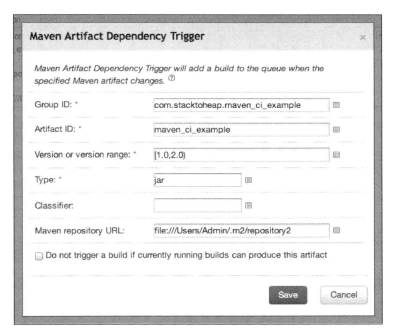

Group ID and **Artifact ID** are the corresponding values that we set in `pom.xml`. **Version range** specifies the versions of the artifact that can be used, in this case between 1.0 and 2.0, with 1.0 inclusive. **Type** specifies the packaging, which is **jar** for our project. Finally, we configure **Maven repository URL** for TeamCity to detect changes that trigger the builds.

Clicking on **Save** adds the build trigger. Now, as the `maven_build` build configuration runs and deploys the distributables to the repository, TeamCity will detect the changes and trigger the `maven_dependant_build` build configuration.

Using Gradle with TeamCity

Gradle is a newer build and deployment automation tool for Java projects. It comes with a rich **Domain Specific Language** (DSL), based on Groovy, to write our build scripts and also to extend Gradle itself.

Installing Gradle

Installing Gradle is similar to installing Ant and Maven. We download the binary distribution, unpack it, and add the bin to the PATH. The commands to install Gradle are as follows:

```
wget http://services.gradle.org/distributions/gradle-1.10-bin.zip
unzip gradle-1.10-bin.zip
export GRADLE_HOME=/usr/local/gradle-1.10
export PATH=$GRADLE_HOME/bin:$PATH
gradle -v
```

 Gradle can also be installed using a package manager on your OS of choice. For example, on Windows, if you are using **Chocolatey**, Gradle can be simply installed using `cinst gradle`.

Building with Gradle on TeamCity

The basic concepts involved in getting a simple build running with Gradle are very similar to those of Ant and Maven. The Gradle build file is usually called `build.gradle`, and builds can be run using `gradle build`. Here, `build` is a Gradle task and is akin to **Targets** in Ant and **Goals** in Maven.

Let's keep it simple with Gradle and have a look at the Gradle build runner that is provided with TeamCity. A view of the settings that are to be configured for the Gradle build runner is shown in the following screenshot:

New Build Step: Gradle |▽

Runner type:	Gradle ▼
	Runner for Gradle projects
Step name:	
	Optional, specify to distinguish this build step from other steps.
Execute step: ⑦	If all previous steps finished successfully (zero exit code) ⬧
	Specify the step execution policy.

Gradle Parameters

Gradle tasks:	▦
	Enter task names separated by spaces, leave blank to use the 'default' task.
	Example: ':myproject:clean :myproject:build' or 'clean build'.
Incremental building:	☐ Enable incremental building
	:buildDependents task will be run on projects affected by changes
Working directory: ⑦	▦ ⬚
	Optional, set if differs from the checkout directory.
Gradle home path:	▦
	Path to the Gradle home directory (parent of 'bin' directory). Overrides agent GRADLE_HOME environment variable
Additional Gradle command line parameters:	▦
	Additional parameters will be added to the 'Gradle' command line.
Gradle Wrapper: ⑦	☐ Use gradle wrapper to build project

Run Parameters

Debug: ⑦	☐ Log debug messages
Stacktrace: ⑦	☐ Print stacktrace

Gradle tasks is where we specify tasks like `build`.

Incremental building can be enabled so that TeamCity can detect the modules changed, and hence trigger the builds only for them. This is similar to the incremental building feature in the Maven runner.

Working directory is the working directory from which the Gradle command is to be executed. **Gradle home path** is the location where Gradle is installed and defaults to the location pointed to by the GRADLE_HOME environment variable.

Additional Gradle command line parameters is used to pass any extra parameters to the Gradle command when needed.

The **Gradle Wrapper** setting can be checked if we want to use the wrapper script to run the builds. This will additionally need the **Path to Wrapper script** to be specified. This is usually checked into the repository and is specified relative to it.

 The Gradle wrapper script (gradlew) makes it very easy even for users who don't have Gradle installed to build the project. The script downloads the necessary version of Gradle needed to start the builds. Using gradlew is identical to using the Gradle command in every other way.

The **Run parameters** section has settings to enable the **Debug** output and **Stacktrace** in the build log, which can be useful to get detailed information on what happened with the builds, especially on failure.

The **Java parameters** and **Code coverage** settings are similar to Ant and Maven runners.

 The system properties passed from TeamCity are available through the teamcity property in Gradle. For example, properties can be accessed by executing teamicty["property_name"].

Introducing database migration tools

As often repeated in this book, maintaining every aspect of getting your application built and deployed to production needs to be maintained in version control. This includes the database too. The database changes need to be integrated pretty much like source code changes.

It is obvious, then, that database definitions and changes are tracked and integrated through files checked into the VCS.

Database migrations make the process of integration the database schema, and the changes made to the database are part of day-to-day development, straightforward, in a CI setup.

When using such tools, migrations are written whenever there are changes to the database. These migrations are like steps needed to move the database from one state to another. They not only perform the change but usually also provide means to roll back the change if needed.

There are many popular database migration tools in the Java world. Flyway is one such example with excellent documentation (`http://flywaydb.org/getstarted/`). Flyway has good integrations with Ant, Maven, and Gradle.

TeamCity does not provide any specific features for database migrations, but with the help of its build runners and other features, TeamCity makes it very straightforward to run database migrations as part of our builds.

Summary

In this chapter, we saw the features that TeamCity provides when it comes to setting up CI for Java-based projects.

Popular Java build and deployment tools, such as Ant, Maven, and Gradle, along with other necessary tools, such as JUnit, JaCoCo and Flyway, were discussed in the context of setting up an ideal CI with TeamCity.

The major takeaway from this chapter is that TeamCity makes it very easy to integrate with our tools of choice. The chapter also came with a caveat that not all features that TeamCity provides need to be used, and some may be against some principles and practices of CI. A balance has to be struck when using these features.

In the next chapter, we will leave the world of Java and enter the world of .NET. We will see that TeamCity is just as feature rich, and powerful, even when it comes to .NET projects.

TeamCity for .NET Projects

5

In this chapter, we will be looking at the various tools present in the .NET ecosystem and also TeamCity's integration with these tools.

We will be covering the following topics in this chapter:

- Using NAnt with TeamCity
- Using MSBuild with TeamCity
- Various ways of integrating the NUnit testing framework with TeamCity
- NuGet support provided by TeamCity
- TeamCity's support for PowerShell and the build tools based on it
- A look at database migration tools for .NET

TeamCity has very rich and high-fidelity integration with .NET-based tools, making it a very appropriate CI tool for teams working with .NET. This chapter will establish this statement as a fact.

Getting started with NAnt on TeamCity

NAnt is a build tool for .NET projects. As can be deduced from the name, it is similar to Ant, which we covered in *Chapter 4*, *TeamCity for Java Projects*. The motivations behind NAnt are the same as that of Ant. For example, like Ant, one of the main motivations for NAnt is to be a cross-platform build tool. NAnt can be used in Windows as well as Unix-based operating systems like Linux.

While Ant itself could be used for .NET projects too, NAnt comes with out-of-the-box support to build .NET projects. Moreover, NAnt can be extended using .NET-based languages that the team might already be familiar with, rather than using Java. Also, obviously, there is no need for a JVM runtime when using NAnt, and only .NET or Mono is required for it.

Installing NAnt

The NAnt distribution can be downloaded from `http://sourceforge.net/projects/nant/files/nant/0.92/nant-0.92-bin.zip/download`.

The ZIP file can be extracted using a tool like 7-Zip or WinRar on Windows. The built-in uncompress utility in Windows Explorer can be used as well. Let's extract NAnt to `C:\nant` for simplicity.

We need the `NAnt.exe` file found at `C:\nant\bin` to be in our PATH environment variable. This can be done from a command line using the following command:

```
setx /m PATH "%PATH%;c:\nant\bin"
```

The command uses `setx` to append the `c:\nant\bin` path to the PATH environment variable.

The command line (cmd or PowerShell) may have to be opened as `Administrator` to perform this change.

Alternatively, the PATH environment variable can be changed using the **Graphical User Interface (GUI)** provided by Windows. It can be accessed from **Control Panel | System** and **Security | System | Advanced System Settings | Environment Variables**.

NAnt can also be installed using Chocolatey by running the command `cinst NAnt`.

On OS X, NAnt can be installed through Homebrew using the command `brew install nant`.

We can open a new cmd window to confirm that the `nant` command is now available.

 For files downloaded from the Internet, Windows may prevent us from executing them for security reasons. From the **Properties** window of such files, we can click on the **Unblock** button to mark files that we trust.

Alternatively, we can use the PowerShell (Version 4.0) cmdlet `Unblock-File` from a PowerShell session to unblock such files. In our case, we can use the following command:

```
Unblock-File c:\nant\bin\*
```

Building NAnt with NAnt

We will use NAnt itself as the sample project to build in this case. The source code of NAnt can be found at `https://github.com/nant/nant`. The source code comes with the `NAnt.build` file that can be used to build NAnt from source.

We can clone the NAnt source code and build from source using the following set of commands:

```
git clone git://github.com/nant/nant.git
cd nant
nant
```

The final `nant` command will pick up the `NAnt.build` file as the build file and run the default target specified within it, which in this case is `test`. This builds NAnt from source and runs tests on it. We can also specify the .NET framework to build against using the `-t` flag. For example, `nant -t:"net-3.5"` will build using the .NET 3.5 framework as the target framework.

The NAnt command-line interface and build files are very similar to that of Ant.

Building on TeamCity

With NAnt being built from source using NAnt on the local workstation, we are ready to start building it from TeamCity.

We can repeat the installation steps for NAnt (binary) on the agent that will run the build. On many projects, we usually just add the NAnt binaries into the repository itself so that it becomes very easy to get started with building using NAnt without having to install it. In Git, it may not be advisable to add binaries to the source code repository. If this is seen as a potential issue, NAnt (and other external tools) may be added to a separate repo, which may then be added as a submodule to the source code repo.

We will begin by creating a new project .NET CI With TeamCity. Then, we can create a new build configuration with the name `nant_build`. Alternatively, we can also copy over one of the build configurations we created previously, such as `ant_build`, and make the necessary changes to the copied version.

In the **VCS Settings** section, we can create and attach a new Git-based VCS root pointing to `git://github.com/nant/nant.git`.

When it comes to adding a **Build Step**, we can choose **NAnt** as the build runner. A view of the resulting settings page that needs to be configured for this runner is shown in the following screenshot:

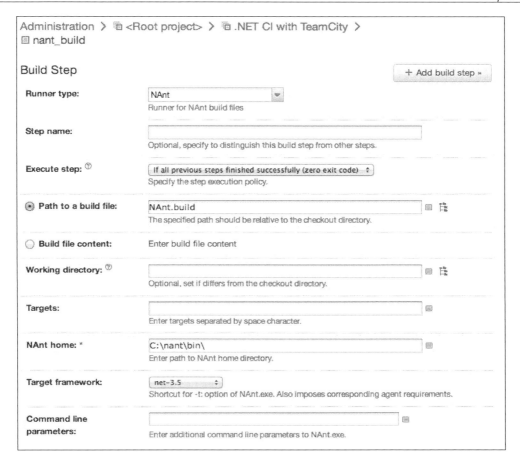

Path to a build file requires the name of the NAnt build file to be run. We specify NAnt.build in this case. Alternatively, we can enter the **Build file content** directly in TeamCity.

Entering build file content directly in TeamCity is not recommended and should be avoided. The build file is supposed to be version controlled with the rest of the source code.

The **Targets** setting is used to specify the targets to be run. We can leave this blank to run the default target specified in the NAnt.build build file.

NAnt home is the directory that contains the NAnt.exe executable. In our case, we specify c:\nant\bin, because c:\nant is the location where we installed NAnt, and the bin folder within it contains the NAnt.exe file.

This setting can also take a relative path, in which case TeamCity will look for NAnt. exe relative to the checked out repository.

We are specifying the **NAnt home** path here pointing to C:\nant for simplicity. For most production uses, it may not be ideal. If the suggestion of checking in NAnt binaries into the source repo is used, then the **NAnt home** path will be relative to the checked out directory.

Alternatively, we can add a property, say nant.home, to the buildAgent.properties file located at <TeamCity agent home directory>/conf and provide the path to NAnt on the agent. With this approach, the agent is able to say where NAnt is configured in it, rather than a person configuring the builds having to know about it. Also, the nant.home property defined here can be set to **Agent Requirement**, thereby ensuring that only agents that do define it are able to run the builds that require NAnt.

Target framework is used to specify the framework to build against, such as net-4.0, net-3.5, mono-2.0, and so on. Using this is equivalent to using the -t flag on the nant command, which we saw previously. We have chosen net-3.5 in this case, as an example.

Additional parameters can be passed to the nant command using the **Command line parameters** setting.

We can also configure coverage for our build configuration using coverage tools such as dotCover, NCover, and PartCover.

We will not be using the coverage features provided by TeamCity as it is better to configure these tools from our build files, rather than through TeamCity. This ensures that developer builds are the same as the builds running on TeamCity.

Details about NCover's extension for NAnt to run code coverage can be found at http://www.ncover.com/support/docs/v3/ref/ nant-extension

We can save the build step to create the nant_build build configuration and trigger it manually to verify that the build is working fine.

Adding NUnit report processing

The build process for the NAnt source also generates NUnit test reports as a part of the test target that is being run as the default. We can configure TeamCity to process these reports and provide more detailed information on the tests that passed and those that didn't in a build. This also enables historical data and statistics involving tests.

The report processing can be added from the **Additional Build Feature** section of the **Build Steps** settings page of the build configuration. The dialog to add **XML report processing** is shown in the following screenshot:

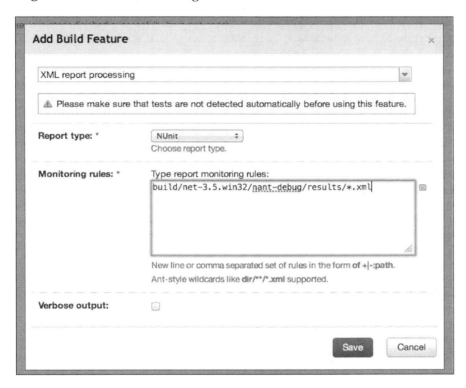

The report type chosen is NUnit as that is the test framework being used through the NAnt build files.

Since the reports were being generated under build/net-3.5.win32/nant-debug/ results/ as multiple .xml files, we have added it under **Monitoring rules**.

We can save the build feature and run the build configuration again to see the test information populated in the build configuration's status message.

Configuring agent requirements

The NAnt build runner automatically adds agent requirements based on the **Target framework** setting. In this case, the runner adds the requirement that the `DotNetFramework3.5.*` parameter (which is any parameter that starts with `DotNetFramework3.5`) should be amongst the parameters defined by the agent. The following screenshot shows the agent requirement added by the NAnt build runner:

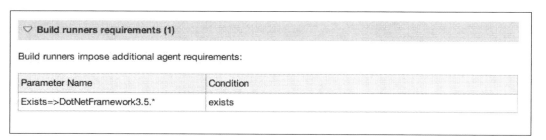

Even if we don't use the NAnt build runner and have to use another runner (like the command-line runner) that does not add such requirements automatically, we can add similar/additional requirements when needed. From the **Agent Requirements** sections of the build configuration, we can click on **Add new requirement** to add requirements.

In this case, we check whether the parameter `DotNetFramework3.5_x86` exists on the agent. We can also add requirements, such as `env.OS` for the agent `equals Windows_NT`. The following screenshot shows the **Agent Requirements** sections with these two requirements set:

Parameter Name	Condition		
DotNetFramework3.5_x86	exists	edit	delete
env.OS	equals Windows_NT	edit	delete

Agent Requirements ⑦
This page lists all requirements that build agents should meet to run your builds.

+ Add new requirement   or pick from frequently used requirements

We can even configure multiple build configurations to build our project against various versions of the framework and even on Mono. The requirement to check whether the OS is `Windows_NT` is superfluous in this case, but is useful if we want to use Mono and run the builds on Windows as well as on Linux/Mac OS X agents.

Building with MSBuild

MSBuild is a build tool/platform for .NET from Microsoft. MSBuild is similar to NAnt in many ways—it uses the XML format for its build files and also has projects, properties, and targets.

But, MSBuild solves one of the biggest cons of using NAnt. With NAnt, the build system that is used in Visual Studio (the de facto IDE for .NET) is very different from that used by the command-line build process. The NAnt build file has no effect on what happens when we perform a build from Visual Studio. With the introduction of MSBuild, however, Visual Studio uses MSBuild to build the projects as well. Thus, .NET projects can now be built in the same manner from Visual Studio as from the command line. Also, since MSBuild is available as a tool independent from Visual Studio, the builds can happen (on CI) without the need for Visual Studio to be installed.

MSBuild build files or project files are the same as the project files that Visual Studio uses (`*.*proj` files).

 Some prefer NAnt to MSBuild because it is not integrated with the IDE. NAnt build files feel more readable and editable, and MSBuild files have the feel that they are to be edited by IDE only (though that is not the case.) In many cases, I have seen a project that has a NAnt build file that calls MSBuild to build the projects and the solutions. Once the assemblies are generated, other NAnt targets perform activities like packaging and deployment.

Installing MSBuild

This is the easiest part when it comes to working with MSBuild. MSBuild comes with the .NET framework, and there is no additional installation required. In many cases, installation of Visual Studio is not needed on the agents and should be avoided. But in complex solutions, especially with web projects, Visual Studio is often a requirement on agent machines too.

Starting with MSBuild 12.0, it is actually not included as part of the framework. MSBuild is available as a separate package, which is also installed along with Visual Studio. The Microsoft Build Tools 2013 package can be found at http://www.microsoft.com/en-us/download/details.aspx?id=40760.

Starting an MSBuild project

As previously mentioned, MSBuild projects are the ones used by Visual Studio. We can create an MSBuild project by creating a project on Visual Studio. As a sample project, I have created a simple C# console application, which can be found at https://github.com/manojlds/msbuild_ci_example.

The project can, of course, be built from Visual Studio from the **Build | Build Solution** menu. The project can also be built from the command line using msbuild.

MSBuild is not present in the path by default. It is located in the root of the framework, for example, at C:\Windows\Microsoft.NET\Framework\v4.0.30319\MSBuild.exe. We can call MSBuild by using this full path or open up the Visual Studio Command Prompt, also called the Developer Command Prompt, where it is automatically added to PATH.

From the root of the project, we can run the msbuild.exe command. MSBuild automatically picks up the solution (.sln) or project file (.*proj) present in the current directory and builds the project. Alternatively, we can also specify the solution or project file explicitly as in the following command:

```
msbuild msbuild_ci_example.sln
```

As is the case with Ant and NAnt, the previous command runs the default target specified in the project. In this case, it is the build target.

Targets to be run can be specified using the /t flag as follows:

```
msbuild msbuild_ci_example.sln /t:clean
```

The previous command cleans the binaries generated from the command before it.

So, we can clean and build our project as follows:

```
msbuild msbuild_ci_example.sln /t:clean;build
```

Alternatively, we can use the rebuild target:

```
msbuild msbuild_ci_example.sln /t:rebuild
```

Building with MSBuild on TeamCity

As expected, TeamCity provides a build runner to run MSBuild projects. Let's create a new build configuration named `msbuild_build` (sorry, following conventions leads to such names at times), and choose MSBuild as the build runner. A view of the necessary settings for this build runner is seen in the following screenshot:

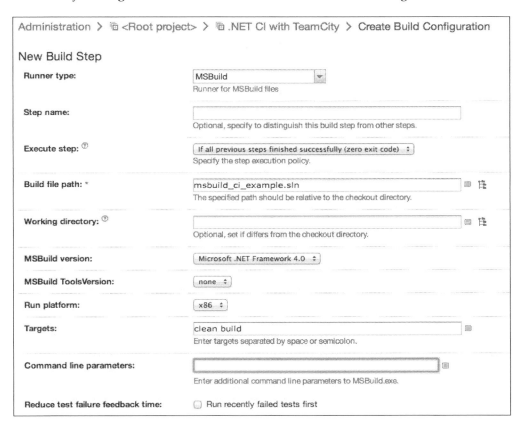

We specify `msbuild_ci_example.sln` as **Build file path**. In this example, **MSBuild version** is chosen as **Microsoft .NET Framework 4.0**.

The **MSBuild ToolsVersion** setting passes the /toolsversion flag to MSBuild and is used to build for older versions using a newer version of the framework. We will leave it as **none** in our case, as the framework version of MSBuild and our project are the same.

Since we want to perform clean followed by build, we specify these as **Targets** to be passed to msbuild.

 The **Rebuild** target (and also the **Rebuild Solution** menu item under **Build** in Visual Studio) performs **Clean** and then **Build**, and can be used instead of specifying the two targets explicitly.

We can further tweak the build runner by passing additional **Command line parameters**, say, for verbose log output. We will ignore the tests and coverage-related options for now and come back to them later.

Let's save the build and run msbuild_build to see if it succeeds.

Adding an NUnit build runner

In the NAnt section, we saw how we can get tighter integration with NUnit using the **XML report processing** feature of TeamCity. TeamCity provides various ways to get such tight integration with NUnit (and other testing frameworks), one of which is a build runner to directly run NUnit tests as part of a build configuration.

From the build steps section of msbuild_build, let's add a new build step and choose **NUnit** as the build runner. The following screenshot shows the settings that need to be configured for this runner:

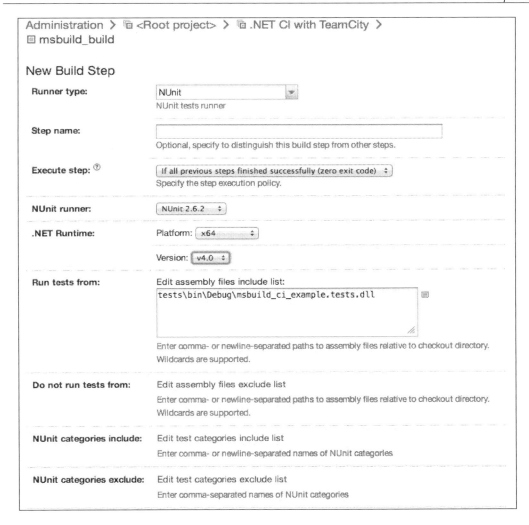

NUnit runner is used to choose the version of NUnit to be used. Here, we choose **NUnit 2.6.2**, which is the latest version, bundled with TeamCity 8.0.4.

.NET Runtime is used to configure **Platform** — 32-bit, 64-bit, or auto, and also the **Version** of the framework. Here, we have configured the runner for 64-bit and Version 4.0 of the framework.

Run tests from is the list of test assemblies to run the tests from. In the sample project, the test project's `.dll` file is created under `tests\bin\Debug\msbuild_ci_example.tests.dll` when we build the solution, and it is this value that we specify for this setting. **Do not run test from** is used to exclude assemblies/directories.

NUnit categories include and **NUnit categories exclude** are used to specify the categories of tests to be run as part of the build.

NUnit categories are used to group tests. Categories can be included and excluded using the `/include` and `/exclude` flags of the NUnit console runner that comes with NUnit. Categories are defined using **Category Attribute**.

One use case for categories is to mark long-running tests so that they can be run as part of a different/parallel build configuration in our CI to keep the builds quick. Another use case would be to mark **Smoke** tests within a fully functional test suite so that only the **Smoke** tests can be run as part of every build.

Run a process per assembly is used to run each assembly in a separate process. This setting may be needed for some test suites to run properly. This is equivalent to setting the `/process` flag of the console runner to **Multiple**.

Reduce test failure feedback time is used to specify whether we want to run tests that failed in the previous build(s) first so that we get quicker feedback if the build is still failing.

In CI, feedback is a key aspect. We want our builds to be fast. If the build is failing, it should fail fast. It is better if the build fails immediately if there is a failure, rather than continuing for a few additional minutes and only then communicating that a failure occurred. From this aspect, running previously failed tests first is a nice feature that we can make use of to get fast feedback on our builds.

Let's save the new build runner and also trigger the build. We should have the test details shown in the status message. Moreover, we will also start getting statistics and historical data about the tests being run in our build.

Compared to the plain **XML report processing** method, this method can report the number of tests that have run successfully/failed much more instantaneously.

Running NUnit tests using NUnit task

MSBuild (like NAnt and Ant) is extensible, and additional tasks can be written for it. One such effort is the MSBuild Community Tasks Project located at `https://github.com/loresoft/msbuildtasks`.

The community project comes with an NUnit task that can be used to run NUnit tests. The community project can be installed in to our test project from the **Package Manager** console using the following command:

```
Install-Package MSBuildTasks
```

Alternatively, the NuGet package can be installed using **Tools | Library package manager | Manage NuGet packages for solution**.

Once installed, we can edit our msbuild_ci_example.tests.csproj file in the sample project, as shown in the following code snippet:

```
<?xml version="1.0" encoding="utf-8"?>
<Project ToolsVersion="12.0" DefaultTargets="UnitTests"
xmlns="http://schemas.microsoft.com/developer/msbuild/2003">
<PropertyGroup>
<MSBuildCommunityTasksPath>$(SolutionDir)\.build</
MSBuildCommunityTasksPath>
<NUnitResultsFile>nunit-results.xml</NUnitResultsFile>
</PropertyGroup>

<Import Project="$(MSBuildCommunityTasksPath)\MSBuild.
  Community.Tasks.Targets" />

  <Target Name="UnitTests" DependsOnTargets="Clean;Build">
    <CreateItem Include="$(OutDir)*.Tests.dll">
      <Output TaskParameter="Include" ItemName="TestAssembly" />
    </CreateItem>
    <NUnit Assemblies="@(TestAssembly)"
      ToolPath="C:\Program Files (x86)\NUnit 2.6.3\bin"
      OutputXmlFile="$(NUnitResultsFile)"
    />
  </Target>
</Project>
```

The previous snippet uses the NUnit task in a target named UnitTests. The UnitTests target is also set as the default target of the project. Now, building the solution will run the tests automatically, and also create the reports file.

We can run the build again with these changes (the sample project repository already has these changes) and see that the tests get executed. With the tests being run directly from MSBuild, we can remove the additional step with the NUnit runner that we added in the previous section. Since the NUnit task is also configured to output the test results report (nunit-results.xml), we can configure **XML report processing** to get tight integration with NUnit tests.

Running NUnit tests using the task provided by TeamCity

There is yet another way to run NUnit tests when using TeamCity. TeamCity ships with a custom task called `NUnitTeamCity` that is very similar to the NUnit task from the community extensions we saw in the previous section. We can make the following modifications to our existing MSBuild project file (`msbuild_ci_example.tests.csproj`):

```
<UsingTask TaskName="NUnitTeamCity" AssemblyFile="$(teamcity_dotnet_
nunitlauncher_msbuild_task)" Condition="'$(TEAMCITY_VERSION)' !=
''"/>


<Target Name="UnitTestsLocal" DependsOnTargets="Clean;Build">
  <CreateItem Include="$(OutDir)*.Tests.dll">
    <Output TaskParameter="Include" ItemName="TestAssembly" />
  </CreateItem>
  <NUnit Assemblies="@(TestAssembly)"
    ToolPath="C:\Program Files (x86)\NUnit 2.6.3\bin"
    OutputXmlFile="$(NUnitResultsFile)"
  />
</Target>


<Target Name="UnitTestsTeamCity" DependsOnTargets="Clean;Build">
  <CreateItem Include="$(OutDir)*.Tests.dll">
    <Output TaskParameter="Include" ItemName="TestAssembly" />
  </CreateItem>
  <NUnitTeamCity Assemblies="@(TestAssembly)"
NUnitVersion="NUnit-2.6.2" />
</Target>


<Target Name="UnitTests">
  <CallTarget Targets="UnitTestsTeamCity
    "Condition="'$(TEAMCITY_VERSION)' != ''"/>
  <CallTarget Targets="UnitTestsLocal"
    Condition="'$(TEAMCITY_VERSION)' == ''"/>
</Target>
```

As seen in the previous code snippet, we create two targets, `UnitTestsLocal` and `UnitTestsTeamCity`, to run the tests on the local developer workstation and TeamCity respectively. The `UnitTestsTeamCity` target uses the custom task `NUnitTeamCity`, provided by TeamCity, to run the tests. This task is loaded using the `UsingTask` task from the location pointed to by the `$(teamcity_dotnet_nunitlauncher_msbuild_task)` property automatically set by TeamCity.

We then create a wrapper target, called `UnitTests`, which runs either the local task or the TeamCity task, based on whether the `TEAMCITY_VERSION` property exists (which won't exist in the local workstation but will be set by TeamCity when running the builds).

We can run the build again with these changes to see that the test information once again gets populated automatically.

We have so far seen multiple ways in which TeamCity provides integration with NUnit. Such ways exist for multiple other tools as well. From one side, this shows the kind of rich integration that TeamCity has with various tools. But, there is a flip side to it as well. Not all the different ways are suitable for proper implementation.

As mentioned in this chapter, and others, the builds should be run the same way between developer boxes and CI. The commands to build a project should be simple and usually involve calling a shell script, batch script, or PowerShell script with some simple arguments. Calling a build tool (`ant`, `nant`, `msbuild`) command directly is usually fine for smaller projects where the command might be straightforward. Such scripts or commands should be the same between CI and the local workstation.

Using the NUnit runner that comes with TeamCity implies that the NUnit tests are not being run the same way as local workstations, as TeamCity uses its own launcher to run the tests. Similarly, using the `NUnitTeamCity` task provided by TeamCity might not be the ideal approach as it brings in a certain degree of dependence on the CI server. The way we have implemented this in the sample project mitigates this to a large extent by running different targets in the local workstation and CI. This difference is a reason not to follow this approach, though it might be a simple implementation in this case.

The preferred way, in the case of NUnit, would be to use the NUnit task that is residing in our project as a library and can therefore be run between the local workstation and CI in the same way. The **XML report processing** feature can be used to get better test result integration.

There might be situations where one approach might be better than the other. The pros and cons might have to be evaluated before going ahead with a particular approach.

Configuring code coverage with MSBuild

Previously, we have seen that the MSBuild runner on TeamCity provides the option to configure code coverage. TeamCity provides out-of-the-box support for dotCover (from JetBrains), NCover, and PartCover through this feature.

We will not be using this feature of TeamCity due to the points mentioned in the previous information box regarding using features that are available only in TeamCity, and not local workstations. Instead, we will be using a coverage tool called OpenCover and configuring it to run through MSBuild.

> A similar setup can be done for the aforementioned coverage tools as well. OpenCover is a free and open source coverage tool for .NET, and it comes with a NuGet package that makes it very easy to configure in our project. OpenCover itself is based on PartCover. More details about OpenCover can be obtained at `https://github.com/OpenCover/opencover/wiki`.

We begin by installing two additional NuGet packages. One is for OpenCover, obviously, and the other is for a library called `ReportGenerator`, which is used to convert the coverage report generated by OpenCover into more readable reports in the form of HTML pages. `ReportGenerator` also supports NCover and PartCover.

The relevant sections of the `msbuild_ci_example.tests.csproj` file that configure coverage for our project are shown in the following piece of code:

```
<PropertyGroup>
<MSBuildCommunityTasksPath>$(SolutionDir)\.build</
MSBuildCommunityTasksPath>
<NUnitResultsFile>nunit-results.xml</NUnitResultsFile>
<NUnit-ToolPath>..\packages\NUnit.Runners.2.6.3\tools\</NUnit-
ToolPath>
<OpenCover-ToolPath>..\packages\OpenCover.4.5.2316\</OpenCover-
ToolPath>
<ReportGenerator-ToolPath>..\packages\ReportGenerator.1.9.1.0\</
ReportGenerator-ToolPath>
</PropertyGroup>

<UsingTask TaskName="ReportGenerator" AssemblyFile="$(ReportGenerator-
ToolPath)ReportGenerator.exe" />
  <ItemGroup>
    <CoverageFiles Include="coverage.xml" />
    <SourceDirectories Include="..\src" />
  </ItemGroup>

<Target Name="Coverage" DependsOnTargets="Clean;Build">
  <Exec Command='$(OpenCover-ToolPath)OpenCover.Console.exe
-register:user -target:$(NUnit-ToolPath)nunit-console-x86.exe
-targetargs:"$(OutDir)msbuild_ci_example.tests.dll /noshadow"
-output:coverage.xml'/>
  <ReportGenerator ReportFiles="@(CoverageFiles)"
TargetDirectory="report" ReportTypes="Html" SourceDirectories="@
(SourceDirectories)" VerbosityLevel="Verbose" />
</Target>
```

In the `Coverage` target, we run the console runner for OpenCover, `OpenCover.Console.exe`, and provide the NUnit console runner, `nunit-console-x86.exe`, as the target to it. This runs the code coverage and generates the `coverage.xml` report. The `ReportGenerator` task, provided by the `ReportGenerator` package, is then used to process these reports into nice, readable HTML reports under the `report` directory.

We can run the build with these changes and check whether the code coverage is being run as part of the build.

> As previously seen in *Chapter 4, TeamCity for Java Projects*, we can upload this `report` directory once it is generated as part of a build on TeamCity as a `coverage.zip` file so that we obtain the **Coverage** tab automatically for our build configuration.

NuGet and TeamCity

We have been mentioning NuGet in passing in previous sections of this chapter. NuGet is a package manager for .NET (and Windows). The client tool of NuGet enables us to create and install packages. The NuGet gallery (`http://www.nuget.org/packages`) is the online feed/repository of NuGet packages. The NuGet extension for Visual Studio allows us to manage NuGet packages for a solution from Visual Studio.

The following screenshot shows the **Manage NuGet Packages** dialog that can be accessed from the **Tools | Library Package Manager | Manage NuGet packages for Solution** menu item:

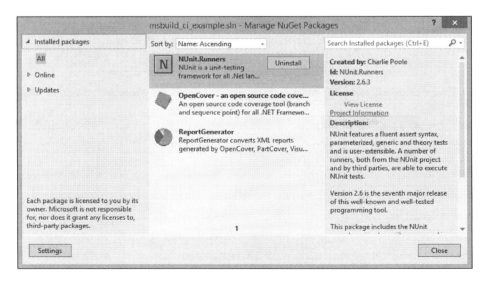

Installing the NuGet command-line client

The NuGet.exe client can be downloaded from http://nuget.org/nuget.exe. The NuGet.exe file can be downloaded and added to PATH as needed.

Installing NuGet.exe on TeamCity agents

TeamCity provides a very simple way to install NuGet.exe on all the applicable build agents. Through this mechanism, we can maintain the NuGet.exe versions on the agents directly from TeamCity in a centralized manner.

From **Administration**, click on **NuGet Settings** under **Integrations** in the left-hand side bar to go to the NuGet-related settings page. There are two tabs, one for **NuGet server settings** and the other for **NuGet.exe**. Let's head to the latter tab to set up NuGet.exe on the build agents.

Click on the **Fetch NuGet** button to choose the version of NuGet.exe to fetch. The following screenshot shows the resulting dialog:

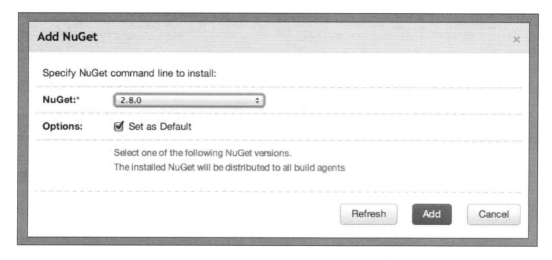

Here, we choose **2.8.0** as the version, the latest at the time of this writing, and also set it as the default NuGet version for use with the various NuGet-related build runners. Click on **Add** to add this version of NuGet.exe.

> The **Upload NuGet** option can be used to upload our own NuGet package containing the NuGet.exe tool. This is useful when we want to use a version that is not visible to TeamCity. Newer NuGet packages for the command-line tool can be obtained from http://www.nuget.org/packages/NuGet.CommandLine.

Once we have added the NuGet version to be used, the `NuGet.CommandLine` package is automatically downloaded from the agents and is ready for use.

TeamCity as a NuGet server

NuGet feeds are essentially repositories of NuGet packages that we want to use in our projects. NuGet Gallery is the public NuGet repository from where we can install packages like `NUnit` and `OpenCover`. For libraries/packages that are internal to our organization, we can maintain our own private feed. There are multiple ways to set up a NuGet repository/feed. NuGet can even work out of a filesystem path or a network share.

TeamCity provides a seamless way to maintain our own NuGet feed. TeamCity does this by doubling as a NuGet feed. When we create NuGet packages as part of our build process, and upload these packages as artifacts of the build configuration, these packages are automatically available through this feed. Now, this feed can be used to install the just-built package in to our project using Visual Studio. We can even use this feed to trigger other builds, which would generally be other projects that are dependent on the just-built packages.

We can now head to the other tab in the **NuGet settings** page: **NuGet server**.

This tab allows us to configure TeamCity itself as a repository/feed for NuGet packages. Clicking on the **Enable** button will make the TeamCity server double as a NuGet feed, as shown in the following screenshot:

TeamCity provides both **Authenticated Feed URL** and **Public Feed URL** to access this NuGet feed. **Public Feed URL** is given only when **Guest User login** is enabled. This feed URL can be used anywhere the NuGet **Gallery Feed URL** is used, including the **Library Package Manager** in Visual Studio.

NuGet-based build runners

TeamCity provides three NuGet-based build runners:

- **NuGet Installer**: This build runner is used to install NuGet packages needed by a project. This is useful for cases where the NuGet packages needed for a project are not checked in to version control.

> Adding all the NuGet packages to version control might not be ideal, especially with VCSs, such as Git and Mercurial. VCSs are generally not good at handling binaries and are meant for source code. However, as it has been mentioned many times in this book, it is ideal to have everything that a project needs to build in version control. The trick is in finding the right balance of tools and libraries that need to be versioned controlled, with others being downloaded as part of the build process or through scripts in a seamless manner.

- **NuGet pack**: This build runner is used to create NuGet packages as part of the build process. NuGet packages can be simply built out of the `.*proj` files or the `.nuspec` files describing the package.

- **NuGet publish**: This build runner is used to publish/push created packages to a NuGet repository/feed.

These NuGet-based build runners make it very easy to perform NuGet-related activities as part of CI. But, the `NuGet.exe` command-line client itself is pretty straightforward, and it is ideal to use the `NuGet.exe` command as part of the build scripts so that the build process is not tied to the TeamCity-provided runners. With the introduction of the **Package restore** features of NuGet, through the NuGet command and through MSBuild tasks, the need for NuGet Installer is obviated.

Due to these reasons, we will not be using the NuGet-based build runners.

NuGet dependency trigger

NuGet dependency trigger can be used to trigger a build when a dependency package is changed in the NuGet feed. This can be useful for monitoring changes to dependencies on external feeds and also on TeamCity's own NuGet package feed.

NuGet dependency trigger works best in Windows with the .NET framework installed. In any other OS, the features are limited. For example, in other OSes, only HTTP-based feeds are supported.

NuGet dependency trigger can be used as an alternative to **Finish build trigger** targeting the build configuration generating the dependency NuGet packages.

Introducing PowerShell

PowerShell is a scripting language with an accompanying command-line shell created by Microsoft to automate tasks on Windows. PowerShell has a strong focus on system administrators. PowerShell has the .NET framework at its core, and hence brings all the features and the excellent library support to system administration activities.

 PowerShell is not just for system administrators. It is for developers too. To stress this point, there is even a book called *Windows PowerShell for Developers*, *Douglas Finke*, *O'Reilly Media*.

With a strong scripting language powered by the .NET framework and its focus on automating tasks, PowerShell makes for a good platform for creating build tools.

PowerShell-based build tools

Psake (`https://github.com/psake/psake`) is a build tool written in PowerShell with the goal of making build automation for .NET projects easier. With the full expressive power of PowerShell, Psake shuns away the XML syntax used in NAnt and MSBuild and is therefore a very flexible and extensible build automation tool.

YDeliver (`https://github.com/manojlds/ydeliver`) is a build and release framework for .NET projects. YDeliver brings in lots of conventions and common tasks needed to get started with the build and release activities of a .NET project. YDeliver builds on the sound foundation provided by Psake.

 Disclaimer: I am the author of the YDeliver framework.

Both Psake and YDeliver are available as NuGet packages on the NuGet gallery, and hence can be easily installed into any project. Since both are PowerShell modules as well, they can be installed and used similar to any other PowerShell module.

PowerShell build runner in TeamCity

TeamCity comes with a PowerShell build runner that can be used to invoke PowerShell scripts, including the build scripts of Psake and YDeliver. The PowerShell build runner can also be seen as an alternative to the command-line build runner to run arbitrary programs. Indeed, PowerShell itself can be seen as a replacement for cmd on Windows.

To illustrate the PowerShell build runner, we will take a YDeliver-based project of mine called cmd (not to be confused with cmd shell on Windows).

 Cmd is a .NET library that aims to make it very simple to run external programs from C# programs. The project can be found at https://github.com/manojlds/cmd.

The project is set up with YDeliver, and we will invoke the YDeliver build script named build.ps1 using the PowerShell build runner on TeamCity.

 PowerShell script files have the extension .ps1. The 1 stood for the version of PowerShell but has not changed even though PowerShell itself has seen four versions to date. This is to maintain backwards compatibility with previous versions of PowerShell.

Let's create a new build configuration named cmd_build and add the PowerShell build runner as a build step. The following screenshot shows a section of the settings needed to configure the runner:

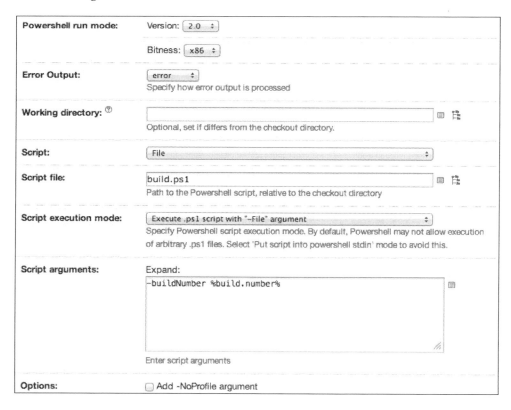

PowerShell run mode is used to define the **Version** and **Bitness** of the PowerShell instance to be used to run the builds. We have chosen to use the 32-bit version of PowerShell 2.0 in this case.

Error Output controls the classification of errors, that is, whether they are to be treated as errors or as warnings.

Script is used to specify whether the PowerShell runner will execute a script provided as a path to a file (specified in **Script file**) or as the content of the file itself (specified in script source).

 Again, as repeated multiple times in this book, it is best to avoid putting whole scripts in TeamCity settings. Such scripts should be version controlled. The **Script Source** option can, however, be used to invoke simple, predefined scripts, module cmdlets, and so on.

Script execution mode decides how the script is to be run through PowerShell. Executing the `.ps1` script with the `-File` argument will run the specified script/content using the `-File` parameter to `powershell.exe`.

The **Put script into PowerShell stdin with -Command** argument passes the script/content into the standard input of Powershell using the `-Command` parameter to PowerShell.

Script Arguments is used to pass additional arguments to the script. In this case, we pass the standard YDeliver parameter, `-buildNumber`, the build number value stored in the `%build.number%` TeamCity parameter.

Adding the `-NoProfile` argument may be used to make PowerShell start up without loading the user profile. This is ideal for builds to ensure that the profile script doesn't affect the build process. It can also speed up the start of the PowerShell process. In this case, we have not selected this option, as we have installed the YDeliver module by importing it on the PowerShell startup through the profile file.

Saving the build and running it should build the `cmd` project on TeamCity as expected.

Database migrations with .NET

In *Chapter 4, TeamCity for Java Projects*, we had an introduction to database migrations and also looked at the flyway tool to manage database migrations.

There are multiple database migration tools available for .NET that follow different approaches towards database migrations.

dbdeploy.net is based on the dbdeploy data migration tool for Java; dbdeploy and dbdeploy.net follow the concept of using SQL-based migrations. It is better to avoid this tool because there are multiple forks of this tool with varying features that have generally not been well maintained.

 Even database migration tools based on Java/JVM, such as dbdeploy and flyway, can be used with .NET projects too, but using a .NET-based one means an additional dependency on something like the JVM is removed.

FluentMigrator (https://github.com/schambers/fluentmigrator/wiki) is another database migration tool. With FluentMigrator, we use C# to write the migrations, rather than SQL. A sample FluentMigrator migration to create a table would look like the following:

```
Create.Table("Users")
    .WithIdColumn()
    .WithColumn("Name").AsString().NotNullable();
```

TeamCity does not provide any special considerations for such database migrations, and they are ideally run using the build tools in an appropriate manner.

Summary

In this chapter, we saw the rich integration that TeamCity provides with various tools in the .NET world. We also saw some of the pros and cons of many of these features from the point of view of the ideal practices for CI.

In my experience, I have found TeamCity to be the best CI server for .NET projects. TeamCity provides first-class integration with major build tools for .NET and also support for multiple tools around testing and code coverage. The NuGet support in TeamCity is unmatched elsewhere.

In the next chapter, we will see that TeamCity is a superstar not just in the .NET world, but is a force to reckon with in the Ruby world too.

6

TeamCity for Ruby Projects

In this chapter, we will look at the various tools involved in setting up CI for Ruby projects. We will be covering **Ruby Version Manager (RVM)**, **rbenv**, **Bundler**, **Rake**, and **RSpec**. We will also look at how these tools come together and integrate with features provided by TeamCity.

Getting started with Rails

Ruby on Rails (or just Rails) is one of the most popular MVC frameworks used to develop web applications. Since Rails requires many of the Ruby tools, such as Bundler and Rake, and comes with a lot of best practices and conventions out of the box, we will use a sample Rails project in this chapter. By using a Rails-based sample project, the idea is to cover the breadth of Ruby (and Rails) support in TeamCity.

The sample project, named `rails_ci_example`, is located on GitHub at `https://github.com/manojlds/rails_ci_example`.

But, before we begin building our sample project, we will take a look at RVM, rbenv, Bundler, and Rake. These common tools are used in most Ruby, and Rails, projects, and an understanding of these is necessary before setting up CI for a Rails project. TeamCity supports all these tools in one form or another.

Managing Ruby versions

Ensuring our Ruby application uses the appropriate Ruby version across developer boxes and also in different environments is very important. Ruby managers, such as **RVM** and rbenv, aim to make this a smooth process.

RVM is not just designed to manage versions of Ruby. In addition to that, it also provides the concept of named gemsets. Gemsets are isolated sets of gems that can be used to get the gems of the corresponding applications alone and nothing else. More information about RVM can be obtained at `http://rvm.io/`.

To install Ruby 2.0.0-p353 using RVM, we can do the following:

```
rvm list known
rvm install 2.0.0-p353
```

The first command is used to list the set of available rubies, and the second is used to install the desired one.

Rbenv is a newer tool, and it aims to simplify the process of managing Ruby versions by focusing on only managing it and nothing else. It does not have the concept of gemsets, and depends on Bundler (discussed in the next section) to handle multiple versions of gems and their dependencies neatly.

> Gemsets are available for rbenv through a plugin, `rbenv-gemset` (`https://github.com/jf/rbenv-gemset`).
>
> The rbenv way, as mentioned, is not to use gemsets like RVM does. It even leaves the management of different versions of gems to Bundler. Not using gemsets means that common gems are not installed again and again across the gemsets. Therefore, using the gemset plugin is not really recommended.

More information about rbenv can be obtained at `https://github.com/sstephenson/rbenv`.

> As an RVM user, I moved to rbenv due to its simplicity and focus. I was also not very supportive of RVM changing the `cd` command to work properly. The rbenv wiki mentions some of these points while discussing why rbenv might be preferred over RVM (`https://github.com/sstephenson/rbenv/wiki/Why-rbenv%3F`).
>
> Either RVM or rbenv should be totally fine from the TeamCity point of view as it has support for both of these tools.

To install Ruby 2.0.0-p353 using rbenv, we can do the following:

```
rbenv install -l
rbenv install 2.0.0-p353
rbenv rehash
```

> The `ruby-build` (`https://github.com/sstephenson/ruby-build`) plugin to rbenv is needed to install different versions of Ruby using the `rbenv install` command. By default, rbenv is not about installing a version of Ruby, but more about managing different versions that can be installed using various different steps/tools.

The first command is used to list all the available versions, and the second one actually installs the necessary version. The rbenv rehash command is used to add all the binaries added from the just-installed Ruby to the PATH through shims.

> The rbenv rehash command must also be rerun whenever a gem is installed, which may expose binaries that may have to be used from the command line.

Introducing Bundler

Bundler helps in managing the dependencies (gems) of an application. In other words, it manages the bundle of gems required by the application.

The list of gems, along with the versions of these gems, is specified in a Gemfile. Bundler can install these gems and handle their dependencies as well. Bundler makes sure that the dependency gems can be loaded for an application without causing any conflicts between different versions of gems.

Gems specified in Gemfile can be installed using the bundle install command. This also creates a Gemfile.lock file, thereby recording the versions of each gem and its dependencies. Together with the Gemfile and Gemfile.lock files, Bundler helps in sharing the same gems for the application across developers and environments.

Installing Rails using Bundler

The following set of commands, as seen in the README file of Bundler, is a good example of getting started with Bundler and also Rails:

```
gem install bundler
bundle init
echo "gem 'rails'" >> Gemfile
bundle install
bundle exec rails new rails_ci_example
```

We install the bundler gem using the gem command. The bundle init command adds a sample Gemfile to the current directory. We add the line gem 'rails' to the generated Gemfile. This marks our intention to install Rails. The bundle install command then installs Rails and its dependencies. This also creates the Gemfile.lock file with the versions of all the necessary gems recorded. We then use the bundle exec command to run rails new and create a new Rails application.

The `bundle exec` command is the way to run a command in the context of the bundle of gems specified in the `Gemfile` and maintained by Bundler.

More information about Bundler can be obtained at `http://bundler.io/`.

Introducing Rake

Rake (Ruby Make) is the most popular build tool in the Ruby ecosystem. The Rake build files, called `Rakefiles`, are written in Ruby.

Rake uses an internal **Domain Specific Language** (**DSL**) in Ruby. DSL is a language developed to solve a particular problem. In the case of Rake, the problem being solved is build-related activities for a project. An internal DSL uses a general-purpose host language (such as Ruby) in a particular way to solve the problem at hand. An external DSL is completely independent of the host language. For example, the configuration management tool Puppet uses an external DSL built and parsed using Ruby.

Just as Ant and NAnt have targets, Rake has tasks as the basic unit of work. `Rakefiles` generally define multiple tasks and can also specify the default task to be run.

When the `rake` command is run in a directory, it looks for `Rakefile` in the current directory, or any of the parent directories. Once `Rakefile` is found, the default task from it is run. Multiple tasks can also be specified from the command line as needed.

All Rails projects come with a standard `Rakefile` to perform various tasks. Gems used in the project can also add more tasks. Custom tasks can be written by adding the `*.rake` files in the `lib/tasks` directory of the Rails application.

The list of Rake tasks available in a Rails or any other Ruby project can be obtained by running `bundle exec rake -T`.

TeamCity provides support for Rake through the Rake build runner, which is what we will use to build our sample project in the next section.

Setting up the build on TeamCity

Let's begin by setting up a new project on TeamCity for this chapter, named `Ruby CI with TeamCity`. We can then add a build configuration named `build` to this project. We can add and attach a new VCS root pointing to `git://github.com/manojlds/ rails_ci_example.git`.

When it comes to adding a build runner, we will choose Rake as the build runner. A view of the settings that need to be configured for this build runner is shown in the following screenshot:

Under **Rake Parameters, Path to a Rakefile** is the path within the source repository to the `Rakefile`. Upon our leaving this empty, the build runner will use the `Rakefile` present in the root of the repository as default, which is what we want.

> Giving a `Rakefile` path here is equivalent to passing the path using the `-f` flag of the `rake` command.

Alternatively, the **Rakefile content** option can be used to specify the contents of the Rakefile in TeamCity.

> The **Rakefile content** feature of TeamCity should be avoided, as it is preferable to have the `Rakefile` version controlled with the source code. This also ensures that what happens on TeamCity is the same as what happens on a local developer workstation.

Working directory is the directory from which the `rake` command is to be executed. Leaving it blank signifies the root of the checked-out repository, which is what we need in this case.

Rake tasks are the set of tasks that we want to run as part of the current build step. For our sample Rails app, we specify the `db:migrate` and `spec:unit` tasks. The `db:migrate` task runs the database migrations if there are any pending migrations.

> Rails has great database migration support out of the box. Rails-like migrations can be used in other Ruby projects using the standalone-migrations gem (`https://github.com/thuss/standalone-migrations`) or similar.

The `spec:unit` task then runs the unit tests that have been written for the Rails application.

> The `spec:unit` task is a custom task written for the Rails application and is located at `lib/spec.rake`. The code that defines the `spec:unit` task is as follows:
>
> ```
> require 'rspec/rails'
> namespace :spec do
>   RSpec::Core::RakeTask.new(:unit) do |t|
>     t.pattern = Dir['spec/*/**/*_spec.rb'].reject{ |f|
> f['/features'] }
>   end
> end
> ```

The Additional Rake command line parameters option can be used to pass additional parameters to the `rake` command if needed. This is left blank in our case.

Under the **Ruby Interpreter** section, **Mode** is used to specify how the build step can find a Ruby interpreter. The different modes are explained as follows:

- The **Default** option uses the interpreter specified by the **Ruby environment configurator** build feature (which we will look at in the coming pages). If the build feature is not specified, the PATH environment variable is used to find the Ruby interpreter.
- The **Path to interpreter** mode is used to specify the path to the Ruby interpreter to be used explicitly.
- The **RVM interpreter** mode is used to specify the Ruby version managed by RVM with an optional RVM Gemset if needed.

We will be using the **Default** mode as it is ideal to separate the interpreter information from the build step. The **Ruby environment configurator** build feature provides this separation neatly, and we will be seeing how we can add that in the next section.

The following screenshot shows the remaining configuration section for the Rake build step:

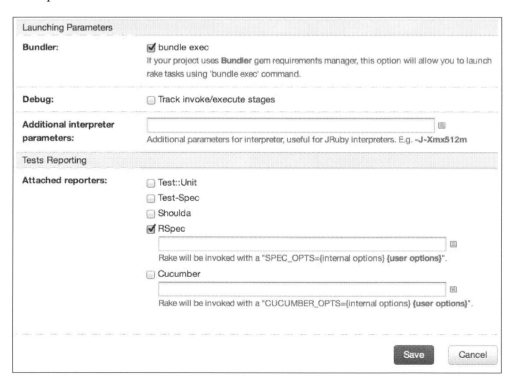

Under **Launching Parameters**, the **Bundler** option is used to check whether the `rake` command is to be run under the context of the current bundle of gems for the application using the `bundle exec` command. This is the preferred way to run Rake and also other tools when using Bundler, as previously explained in the Bundler section.

Debug is used to enable additional information about the tasks being run. **Additional interpreter options** is used to pass parameters to the Ruby interpreter itself.

Under **Tests Reporting,** we have the ability to choose one or more Test frameworks whose reports are to be handled by TeamCity as part of the build step. Teamcity supports **Test::Unit, Test-Spec, Shoulda, RSpec**, and **Cucumber out of the box**.

We will use RSpec in the sample application to run all the tests, and hence we'll only enable it for test reporting.

 Some projects need to enable, for instance, RSpec and Cucumber as the feature tests may be written using Cucumber.

We can save the build step and move on to configuring the Ruby interpreter for the build configuration.

Setting up Ruby interpreter

As mentioned in the previous section, the **Ruby Interpreter Configurator** is a build feature that can be added to any build configuration that is dependent on a Ruby interpreter. This build feature is used to specify the location of the Ruby interpreter, so that the Rake build runner can use it when it is configured in **Default** mode.

After saving the rake build step, we can add a new build feature from the **Build Steps** section by clicking on the **Add Build Feature** button. Here, we will choose **Ruby environment configurator** as the feature to add.

The Configure Ruby environment for build steps via option has three methods to specify the interpreter:

- **Path to Ruby Interpreter**: In this method, the interpreter path is specified explicitly, such as `/usr/bin/ruby`.

- **RVM**: This method can be used when RVM is used to maintain Ruby versions and isolate the gems for an application. With this method, the Ruby interpreter version as managed by RVM, along with an optional RVM gemset can be mentioned. The gemset can also be created by TeamCity if it doesn't already exist.

Alternatively, `.rvmrc`, the RVM configuration file for the project, can be used to configure the RVM-managed Ruby interpreter. Using RVM adds an implicit agent requirement for the `RVM_PATH` environment variable. This can also be added to the build parameters if it's not set as an environment variable on the agent.

The dialog to add **Ruby Interpreter Configurator** using RVM is shown in the following screenshot:

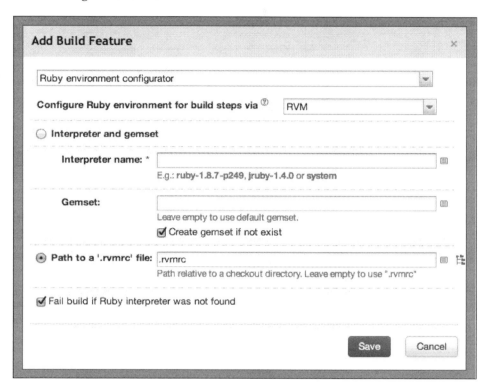

- **rbenv**: When using rbenv to manage Ruby versions, this option can be used. Similar to RVM, this option needs the interpreter version to be specified. Alternatively, the path to the `.rbenv-version` file can be specified to get the version from it.

  Using rbenv adds an implicit agent requirement for the `RBENV_ROOT` environment variable to be set on the agent. This can also be added as a build parameter if needed.

The dialog to add **Ruby Interpreter Configurator** using rbenv is shown in the following screenshot:

The latest version of rbenv as of this writing, 0.4.0, uses .ruby-version as the Ruby version file. It still supports .rbenv-version file for backwards compatibility.

The .ruby-version file can also be used with RVM to specify the Ruby version and can be seen as an alternative to using .rvmrc. TeamCity 8.1 supports .ruby-version file usage.

The Fail build if Ruby interpreter was not found option can be enabled to fail the build if TeamCity is unable to find the Ruby interpreter if the interpreter cannot be found using the configured method.

Save the build feature to add it to the build configuration.

We can now run the `build` build configuration to see it pass.

Running Capybara- and Selenium-based feature tests

We can also add a `features` build configuration to run the Capybara- and Selenium-Webdriver-based feature tests present in the sample project. The feature tests can be run by using the rake task `unit:features`.

> Capybara is a Ruby gem that provides a DSL for functional testing web applications. It works with `Rack::Test` and `Selenium` drivers. Capybara can be used with the RSpec, Cucumber, and Test::Unit frameworks.
>
> More details about Capybara can be obtained at `https://github.com/jnicklas/capybara`.

The task spins up an instance of the application and runs the tests against it. It is also possible to deploy the app to Heroku in a separate build configuration and run the tests against the deployed version just as we did in *Chapter 3, Getting Your CI Up and Running*.

> There is also a Heroku headless (`https://github.com/jnicklas/capybara`) gem that can be used to deploy applications to Heroku without having to handle Git remotes and `ssh` keys on the agent.

Summary

In this chapter, we had a look at the support that TeamCity has for Ruby projects. Through the Rake runner, and the ability to specify a Ruby interpreter through RVM and rbenv, TeamCity has most Ruby projects covered.

We also saw that TeamCity supports the most common testing frameworks for Ruby projects such as RSpec and Cucumber, thereby simplifying test report processing immensely.

In the next chapter, we will be looking at how TeamCity supports mobile projects, as well as other technologies such as Node.js.

7
TeamCity for Mobile and Other Technologies

After having covered CI for some major platforms and technical stacks, such as Python, Java, .NET, and Ruby in the previous chapters, in this chapter we will be looking at how TeamCity fares when it comes to mobile projects, specifically Android and iOS projects.

Also, we will be taking a look at some plugins for TeamCity and how they extend TeamCity to provide first-class support for even more platforms, such as Node.js.

CI for Android projects

TeamCity has no special support to build **Android** projects primarily because the tooling is very similar to other Java projects. Android projects generally use Maven or Gradle as the build tools, both of which were covered in *Chapter 4*, *TeamCity for Java Projects*. In this section, we will take a look at setting up the CI for a sample Gradle-based Android application.

The sample application that we will use is `Android_CI_Example` located at `https://github.com/manojlds/android_ci_example`.

> The sample application was created using the Android Studio IDE. Android Studio is an IDE focused on Android development based on the IntelliJ IDEA platform (from Jetbrains). As of this writing, the IDE is still in Early Access Preview and has a few kinks to be worked out. More details about Android Studio can be obtained at `http://developer.android.com/sdk/installing/studio.html`.

Generating the APK

We will begin by creating a new project named `Android CI for TeamCity`. Next, we will add a build configuration named `build`. The **VCS Root** for the configuration has to be configured to point to `git://github.com/manojlds/Android_CI_Example.git`.

For the **Build Runner**, we will choose **Gradle**. We will use `clean build` as the Gradle tasks. The tasks, in short, compile the code, run unit tests, and generate the **Android Application Package (APK)** for the application.

 The sample application uses the **Robolectric** (`http://robolectric.org/`) unit-testing framework for the unit tests. The frameworks help in keeping the unit tests fast by running the tests in the JVM and also remove direct dependency on the Android SDK and the Android emulator.

The APK for the application is generated under `Android_CI_Example/build/apk` from the root of the repository. We will configure this path as the Artifacts path and publish the APK as an artifact of this build configuration as shown in the following screenshot:

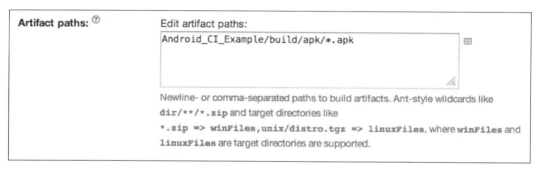

The Gradle tasks also need the `ANDROID_HOME` environment variable to be set pointing to the Android SDK directory to work properly. We can add this environment variable from the **Build Parameters** section of the build configuration.

 In a much more real-world setup, it is ideal to add a property pointing to the Android home in the `buildAgent.properties` file located at `<TeamCity Agent Home Directory>/conf`. This way, the agents can communicate with the Android home rather than having an administrator configure it in the build configuration settings.

This is especially useful when agents are built through infrastructure automation.

After creating the build configuration, we can run the build to see it pass. The test information should be automatically populated on TeamCity, and the APK must be uploaded as well.

Running Calabash tests

Now that our APK is generated, it is time to run some functional tests against it. For our sample app, we will be using Calabash (`https://github.com/calabash/ calabash-android`) as the functional testing framework. The tests are present in a separate repo located at `https://github.com/manojlds/Android_CI_ Example_Calabash`.

 Calabash is a Ruby gem, and the tests are written in Ruby. The test project can be set up by first running `bundle install` to install the necessary gems.

Once the APK (`Android_CI_Example-debug-unaligned.apk`) is obtained by building the app, the Calabash tests can be run by executing the following commands:

```
calabash-android resign apk/Android_CI_Example-debug-unaligned.apk

calabash-android run apk/Android_CI_Example-debug-unaligned.apk --format
pretty --format html -o android_report.html
```

 The `calabash-android resign` command helps in signing the APK. More detail can be found here: `https://github.com/ calabash/calabash-android/wiki/Running-Calabash- Android`.

Note that we will generate an HTML report, named `android_report.html`, while running the tests.

Let's configure these Calabash tests on TeamCity. We begin by adding a `calabash-tests` build configuration with **VCS Root** pointing to `git://github.com/manojlds/Android_CI_Example_Calabash.git`.

We will use the command-line runner to run the Calabash-based tests. We need to specify the `ANDROID_HOME` environment variable under **Build Parameters** for this build configuration as well.

> Alternatively, we can also set the `ANDROID_HOME` parameter on the project itself, rather than setting it in both the build configurations.

We will fetch the APK generated in the previous build and use it for the tests. For this, we will set up **Artifact Dependencies** and **Snapshot Dependencies** on `build` for the `calabash-android` build configuration as shown in the following screenshot:

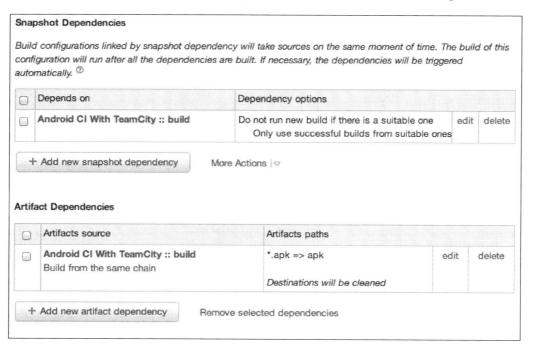

In this setup, Calabash finds the connected devices/emulators and runs the tests against the application deployed on them. For CI, here we are assuming that an emulator/device is always connected, ready to run the tests. A more complex scenario might involve spinning up the emulators on demand, running the tests, and stopping them again.

> The IntelliJ IDEA project runner is also a good choice to build Android applications that are built as IntelliJ IDEA projects.

Building iOS projects on TeamCity

TeamCity comes with the Xcode Project build runner to build Xcode projects. We can leverage this runner to build iOS projects. To illustrate the Xcode Project build runner in this section, we will use AnyWall (`https://github.com/ParsePlatform/AnyWall`) as the sample application.

> An Xcode project can be built from the command line using the following command:
>
> ```
> xcodebuild -project AnyWall.xcodeproj -target Anywall
> -configuration Debug -sdk iphonesimulator7.0 clean
> build
> ```
>
> `AnyWall.xcodeproj` is the project file. `AnyWall` is the target application to be built, in the `Debug` configuration. Since we want to build for the iOS simulator, we specify `iphonesimulator7.0` as the SDK. Here, `clean` and `build` are the actions to be executed.

Let's start off by creating a new project named iOS CI with TeamCity. Then, we can create a build configuration named build with **Xcode project** chosen as the build runner for it. A view of the settings needed for the Xcode project build runner is shown in the following screenshot:

For **Path to the project or workspace**, we specify AnyWall.xcodeproj as the project file. Under **Build Settings**, we can click on the **Check/Reparse Project** button so that TeamCity can parse the project file and gather information about the project.

For the **Build** setting, we can choose either the **Target-based** or **Scheme-based** build. For the **AnyWall** app, we will be using the **Target-based** build to build the project.

A target in Xcode is the application to be built from the project. A scheme is a collection of targets to build, along with the necessary configuration to build them.

The **Target** can be left as **<Default>** or changed to **AnyWall** (automatically populated by TeamCity after parsing the project), which is the actual target application that we want to build. Configuration can be set to **Debug** to perform a debug build.

We will use **Simulator-iOS** as the **Platform** and **Simulator-iOS 7.0** as the **SDK**. **Architecture** can be left as **<Default>**. We can also choose other architectures as needed, such as **i386**, **arm7**, and so on.

Build action(s) are tasks that need to be executed as part of the build. By default, it is populated as **clean build**, and we can leave it as such. We can also enable **Run Tests** if we want to run the tests present in the project as part of the build.

The **Additional command line parameters** setting can be used to send parameters/arguments to the project.

We can save the build and run it to see it pass.

 Just like the Android app, Calabash can be used to run functional tests for iOS applications as well. More details are available at `https://github.com/calabash/calabash-ios`.

So far, we have seen how TeamCity can lend us a hand for Android and iOS projects. While TeamCity comes with a lot of features out of the box, TeamCity can also be extended through a number of plugins that make the job of setting up CI easier. In the upcoming sections, we take a look at a few plugins that are available for TeamCity for use with different platforms and technology stacks.

Installing TeamCity plugins

TeamCity has a plethora of plugins that can be used to extend and simplify the way TeamCity works. Many of the functionalities/features of TeamCity that come out of the box are in fact plugins that are bundled with TeamCity. These bundled plugins begin their life as external plugins that have to be installed, and then became bundled due to their usage and usefulness.

 Most of the plugins available for TeamCity are listed at `http://confluence.jetbrains.com/display/TW/TeamCity+Plugins`.

The list of bundled plugins in a TeamCity server can be seen from **Administration | Plugins List** as shown in the following screenshot:

This TeamCity installation has **72** plugins
Available plugins

Bundled plugins

Plugin Name	Version	Vendor	Home Path
.NET build runners support	27616	JetBrains, s.r.o.	<WEB-INF>/dotNetRunners
Agent System Info Provides agent system information	27616	JetBrains, s.r.o.	<WEB-INF>/.unpacked/agentSystemInfo
Amazon EC2 Support Support for build agents running on Amazon EC2	27616	JetBrains, s.r.o.	<WEB-INF>/cloud-amazon
Ant network tasks	27616	JetBrains, s.r.o.	<WEB-INF>/ant-net-tasks
Apache Ant distribution rebundled by JetBrains	27616	JetBrains, s.r.o.	<WEB-INF>/ant-tool
Apache Ant runner support	27616	JetBrains, s.r.o.	<WEB-INF>/ant
Bugzilla integration	27616	JetBrains, s.r.o.	<WEB-INF>/bugzilla
Build Agent JVM updater	27616	JetBrains, s.r.o.	<WEB-INF>/jvm-update
Code Coverage (Java) Support for Java code coverage (uses IntelliJ IDEA or EMMA)	27616	JetBrains, s.r.o.	<WEB-INF>/coverage
Command Line	27616	JetBrains, s.r.o.	<WEB-INF>/commandLineRunner
dotnet-tools Introduced R# inspections runner and .NET duplicates finder	27616	JetBrains, s.r.o.	<WEB-INF>/.unpacked/dotnet-tools
Duplicates Finder (Java) Finds and reports duplicates in Java code	27616	JetBrains, s.r.o.	<WEB-INF>/Duplicator
Eclipse Plugin Distributor Included Eclipse Plugin into TeamCity installation	27616	JetBrains, s.r.o.	<WEB-INF>/.unpacked/eclipse-plugin-distributor
External Change Viewers	27616	JetBrains, s.r.o.	<WEB-INF>/changeViewers

The general steps involved in installing a plugin to TeamCity are:

1. Stop the TeamCity server.

2. Copy the zipped plugin to `<TeamCity Data Directory>/plugins` (`TeamCity Data Directory` is the directory where the TeamCity server's data is installed as mentioned in *Chapter 2, Installation*).

3. Start the TeamCity server. TeamCity will decompress the plugin and start using it if everything is fine with the plugin.

That's it! It is obvious that installing plugins to TeamCity is very simple.

Installing the Python runner plugin

In *Chapter 3, Getting Your CI Up and Running*, we had set up the CI for a Python project. In that setup, we used the command-line runner for all the build steps. There is also the Python runner available as a plugin that could have been used for the steps involving Python scripts.

 The Python runner plugin is able to detect the installed Python runtimes in the agent and also sets the path to the Python interpreter. Thus, it is possible for us to automatically detect the Python runtimes in an agent and also ensure that Python builds are run in compatible agents only. This is the main advantage over using the command-line runner option.

The Python runner plugin can be downloaded from `https://code.google.com/p/teamcity-python/`. The downloaded ZIP file has a version number appended to the name. Let's rename it to just `python.zip`.

The TeamCity server has to be stopped for a clean plugin installation as mentioned in the beginning of this section. We will stop the server as per the platform-specific instructions provided in *Chapter 2, Installation*.

Now, we can copy over the `python.zip` plugin to `<TeamCity Data Directory>/plugins`.

We can start the server now, again by referring to the instructions from *Chapter 2, Installation*.

Once the server is started, we will notice that TeamCity has decompressed the plugin under `<TeamCity Data Directory>/plugins/.unpacked/python`. We can also confirm that the plugin is installed by going to **Administration | Plugins List** and looking for the plugin under the **External plugins** section as shown in the following screenshot:

This TeamCity installation has **73** plugins (including 1 external)
Available plugins

External plugins

Plugin Name	Version	Vendor	Home Path
Python runner	1.0.84.138	Leonid Bushuev	<TeamCity Data Directory>/.unpacked/python

Bundled plugins

Plugin Name	Version	Vendor	Home Path
.NET build runners support	27616	JetBrains, s.r.o.	<WEB-INF>/dotNetRunners
Agent System Info Provides agent system information	27616	JetBrains, s.r.o.	<WEB-INF>/.unpacked/agentSystemInfo

Building with the Python build runner

In *Chapter 3, Getting Your CI Up and Running*, the build step for running unit tests used the command-line runner to run the following command:

```
python manage.py test polls --with-coverage --cover-package=polls
--cover-html --with-xunit
```

We will move from the command-line runner to the Python runner for this build step.

We can begin by deleting or disabling the existing build step to run the unit tests. Then, we will add another **Build Step** and choose the newly installed **Python** build runner. A view of the settings that have to be configured for this build runner is shown in the following screenshot:

The **Python kind** setting is used to choose between the CPython (**Classic Python**) version, **Iron Python**, and **Custom Python**. We choose **Classic Python** and **2.x** as the version (since we are targeting 2.7.5).

Bitness, as the name suggests, is used to choose between 32-bit (**x86**) and 64-bit (**x64**) for the runner. We choose **x64** in our case. **Python executable** is set to the auto configuration parameter `%Python.2.x64%` (based on the previous settings.) The Python runner plugin helps in automatically detecting installed python in the agents and sets the parameter to the Python path. Hence, adding the build runner also adds an implicit **Agent Requirement** for this property.

> The `%Python.2.x64%` parameter can be changed from the **Build Parameters** section if needed.

The **Script** option can be used to choose between **File** and **Source code** for the runner. **File** is the preferred option as we would want to run the build using a file in version control, rather than some arbitrary source code known only to TeamCity. The **Python file** setting is used to specify the file that needs to be run using Python and **Command line arguments** mentions the arguments to be passed to this file.

We can save the build runner and run the build again to see it pass.

> Why use the Python runner over the command-line runner? After all, the command-line runner can be used to trigger the scripts directly using python. The Python runner is a convenience feature as it allows us to choose the Python version easily and automatically detects the location of that version on the agents. By adding implicit agent requirements, the runner ensures that only the agents that do have the specified Python can run the build configuration. Using the command-line runner, such requirements have to be added manually.
>
> Such arguments against a more specific runner versus the command-line runner can be made for most of the runners. These runners help in simplifying the setup, and if all else fails, the command-line runner should always be handy.

Introduction to TeamCity.Node plugin

There is also the `TeamCity.Node` plugin to TeamCity that brings in support for Node.js and related tools, such as Grunt and NPM, to TeamCity. The plugin can be downloaded using the instructions provided at `https://github.com/jonnyzzz/TeamCity.Node`.

 Node.js is a framework to develop applications using JavaScript. It is based on the Chrome V8 JavaScript engine. More details can be obtained at `http://nodejs.org/`.

The plugins come with few runners to make setting up builds for Node.js projects simpler, as follows:

- **Grunt**: This is used to run Grunt tasks
- **Node.js**: This is used to run a JavaScript source file or code directly specified in the runner
- **Node.js NPM**: This is used to execute NPM commands, such as `npm install`
- **Node.js NVM Installer**: This is used to manage the version of Node.js using **Node Version Manager (NVM)**, based on RVM
- **Phanthom.JS**: This is used to execute JavaScript or coffeescript source code or files using the Phantom.JS runtime

 Grunt is a JavaScript-based build tool and task runner to automate tasks for a project. Grunt is not limited to Node.js, and can be used for any project.

Grunt is perhaps the most essential build runner amongst these (as Grunt tasks can in turn be configured to do the job of other build runners). The following screenshot shows a view of the settings for the Grunt build runner:

New Build Step

Runner type:

Grunt

Executes Grunt tasks

Step name:

Optional, specify to distinguish this build step from other steps.

Execute step: ⓘ

If all previous steps finished successfully (zero exit code) ⬍

Specify the step execution policy.

Grunt:

NPM package from project ⬍

Specify weather you like to use system-wide or project's npm installed grunt

Grunt File:

Specify grunt file path relative to checkout directory. Leave blank to use Gruntfile.{js,coffee}

Grunt Tasks:

Commands:

Specify grunt tasks to run (new-line separated)

Working directory: ⓘ

Optional, set if differs from the checkout directory.

Additional command line parameters:

Expand

Enter additional command line parameters for Grunt. Put each parameter on a new line

The settings are pretty similar to that of many other runners we have seen so far.

> Just like the Python runner plugin, the TeamCity.Node plugin also helps in detecting the path to Node.js and npm CLI tools and adds these as configuration properties on the agent. This also ensures that only agents with these tools are able to run the build configurations that need them.

The Python runner plugin and TeamCity.Node plugin are just examples of plugins that can be put to good use. There are plugins that add support for additional VCS, more testing frameworks, issue trackers, runners, and even change the TeamCity user interface.

There are some plugins that are very innovative too. For example, the Artifacts Torrents plugin (http://confluence.jetbrains.com/display/TW/Torrent+plugin), available in TeamCity 8.1+, turns the server into a Torrent tracker, and the agents into seeds to download artifacts above 10MB in size. This is extremely valuable in large installations as this reduces the load on the server when lots of agents are downloading many large files at the same time.

We will also be looking at a few other plugins in detail in the upcoming chapters.

Summary

In this chapter, we began by looking at how TeamCity can be used for mobile projects, such as Android and iOS.

We then went on to install and use plugins that extend TeamCity to provide features that are not available out of the box. We looked at the Python build runner and TeamCity.Node plugins that immensely improve the support for Python and Node.js projects in TeamCity. Various other plugins also add such support to other platforms and technology stacks.

In the next chapter, we will be looking at how TeamCity integrates with other tools such as IDEs, issue trackers, GitHub, and more.

8
Integration with Other Tools

In this chapter, we will look at the kind of integrations that TeamCity has with various other tools. Such integrations enable developers and other members of the team to easily stay on top of what's happening on CI.

More specifically, we will be looking at the following tools and how TeamCity can be integrated with them:

- IDE integrations for IntelliJ platform plugins and Visual Studio that enable developers to track and monitor builds right in the comfort of their IDEs
- Issue tracker support that enables easy tracking of issues/stories/bugs that have been addressed in builds
- Integrations that make it all the more easy to work with GitHub
- Build monitor and other information dissemination plugins/tools

IDE integrations

TeamCity provides powerful integrations with many major IDEs that help to make the process of running, monitoring, and examining CI builds a seamless experience. These integrations help developers to work with TeamCity without having to ever leave their IDEs.

The supported IDEs include IntelliJ-based IDEs, Visual Studio, and Eclipse.

IntelliJ platform IDEs integration

As expected, TeamCity provides support for IDEs based on the IntelliJ platform (IntelliJ IDEA, RubyMine, PyCharm, and more).

We will take the `django_ci_example` Django project used in *Chapter 3*, *Getting Your CI Up and Running*, as an example to demonstrate integrations with PyCharm IDE.

Installing the plugin

Plugins for PyCharm can be installed from the **Preferences | IDE Settings | Plugins** window. Here, click on **Browse repositories** and search for TeamCity. The **TeamCity Integration** plugin must be listed. We can double-click on the listed plugin to download and install it.

To activate the plugin, we need to restart the IDE. Once the IDE is restarted, TeamCity should be available as a menu item. The first order of business is to log in to the TeamCity server. This is done by clicking on **TeamCity | Login** and providing the authentication details in the resulting dialog, as shown in the following screenshot:

 Once the login has been done and a communication with the server has been established, it is ideal to update the plugin to the version built for the TeamCity version we have connected to. This is easily done by using the **TeamCity | Update plugin** menu item.

The plugin can alternatively be downloaded directly from the TeamCity server, from the **My Settings and Tools** page (accessed by clicking on the logged-in username in the top-right corner). The download/installation links for various plugins are provided in the **TeamCity Tools** box, as shown in the following screenshot:

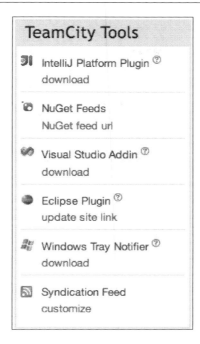

Configuring notifications

Using **TeamCity** | **Options** | **Edit Notification Rules**, we can set the kind of notifications sent to our IDE. Clicking on this menu item opens up the **Notification Rules** tab in the **My Settings & Tools** page that we just discussed.

 Default notification rules are set for all users to notify them when a build fails with their changes. TeamCity identifies the changes of a user by using the username set in **Version Control Username Settings** found in the **My Settings & Tools** page.

We can add our own notification rules as needed, such as monitoring events in a particular project/build configuration. The following screenshot shows an example of a build failure notification:

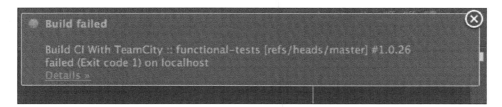

Managing projects from the IDE

The plugin also enables us to have a quick look at the projects concerned, our changes, the investigations assigned to us, build failures logs, and so on. The following screenshot shows a sample status of the TeamCity plugin window:

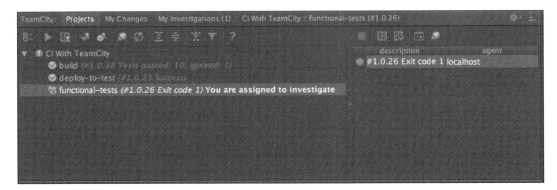

As seen from the screenshot, it is possible to queue build configurations, mark an investigation as fixed, and also look at the builds in more detail by opening up the project in the TeamCity web UI.

Opening files and patches in IDE

For VCS changes and files within them, TeamCity provides links to open them in IDE, as shown in the following screenshot:

Clicking on the **IDE** link opens up the concerned file in the (active) IDE. In the case of entire changes, the patches are downloaded to the IDE, and they can be applied to the working directory as required.

Remote Run

Remote Run (also called Personal Build) is a feature that makes the IDE integrations all the more useful. With this feature, it is possible to run the build for local changes that haven't even been committed/pushed to the VCS repository.

 The use case for the Remote Run feature is to make sure that the changes we are about to push to the repository do not break the build. We can safely perform Remote Run with our changes and see how they are integrated with other changes in the repository. Once we are sure that the build is successful, we can then push our changes to the repository.

Remote Run can be triggered by using the **TeamCity | Remote Run** menu item. This brings up a dialog where we can select the local changes to be run. Clicking on the **Run in TeamCity...** button in this dialog brings up the dialog to choose the build configurations to be run for this change, as shown in the following screenshot:

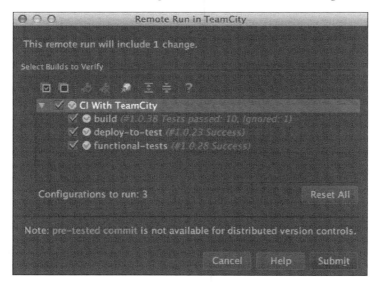

Here, we have chosen all the build configurations in the CI With TeamCity project. Clicking on **Submit** will trigger personal builds on these build configurations for the selected local changes.

 There is also the **TeamCity | Remote Run Outgoing changes** option available. This differs from the normal Remote Run option in that the changes have already been committed, but not yet pushed to the remote repository. In Remote Run, the changes have not even been committed yet.

The Remote Run feature is useful to see how the local changes integrate with the existing sources. Instead of running the build on the local machine, the build is triggered directly on the TeamCity server itself to see how it fares. Failed builds only give feedback on the local change for the user, but will not affect the normal builds. The Remote Run builds are also visible to only the user that initiated the builds.

>
> The Remote Run feature can be used in cases where a build runs faster on TeamCity (agent) than the local developer workstation. Care must be taken to ensure that the available agents are not constantly used up for personal builds, thereby queuing up the normal builds for long periods of time.
>
> The feature may have to be used prudently, and not as a complete replacement for dev builds on local workstation.

Pre-tested (delayed) commit is a feature that builds on the Remote Run feature. After the personal builds for a Remote Run are done, the IDE plugin also commits the pre-tested commit and sends the changes to the repository. It can be enabled from the Remote Run dialog by choosing the **Commit changes if successful** option.

The Branch Remote Run trigger is an allied feature to Remote Run. It is a build trigger that can be added to build configurations that we want to support personal builds for. With this trigger set, developers can push their changes to a branch (located at `refs/heads/remote-run/<branch_name>` for Git.) TeamCity looks at the predefined location for such remotely-run branches and triggers personal builds for the user.

At the time of writing this, the Branch Remote Run trigger is supported for Git- and Mercurial-based build configurations only. Feature branches support extends this concept to build branches through non-personal builds. We will be taking a detailed look at feature branch support in TeamCity in *Chapter 11*, *Beyond CI – Continuous Delivery*.

Visual Studio integrations

The TeamCity Visual Studio add-in provides tight integrations between the IDE and TeamCity.

The add-in can be downloaded from the **My Settings & Tools** page using the **Visual Studio Addin download** link in the **TeamCity Tools box**. The installation steps for the MSI are pretty straightforward and also enable the integration of the addin with multiple versions of Visual Studio.

The experience is pretty similar to the integration for IntelliJ platform IDEs, but it is not as feature rich as the latter. There is no straightforward way to look at projects, and there are no notifications through Visual Studio.

Once the add-in is installed, the **TeamCity** menu item is available in Visual Studio.

After the login details are set up, Remote Run, My Changes, My Investigations, and other IDE integrations are available, much like what we saw in PyCharm.

 The addin for Visual Studio does not support Remote Run for Git and Mercurial. An alternate way of doing it is available through Branch Remote Run trigger, which we saw in the previous section.

The following screenshot shows the **My Investigations** window, with the `msbuild_ci_example` project being investigated:

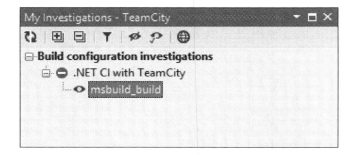

GitHub integrations

All the projects that we have built so far use GitHub as the Git repository host. Creating VCS roots based on GitHub and polling the repository for changes is the same as using any other Git host.

However, TeamCity can provide much tighter integration with GitHub, which is what we will look at in this section.

GitHub webhooks and services

GitHub provides integrations with various third-party tools. These integrations help to trigger different actions in these third-party tools based on the activity—such as pushing to a repository—on GitHub.

TeamCity is one such third-party tool that GitHub supports. With the third-party services integration enabled, we can have GitHub trigger builds when there is a push, rather than have TeamCity poll the repository for changes.

The integration can be enabled from the **Settings | Webhooks & Services** page for the repository concerned on GitHub. Click on the **Configure services** button to get a list of the supported third-party tools, and choose **TeamCity** from the list. The settings that have to be configured to enable push triggering are shown in the following screenshot:

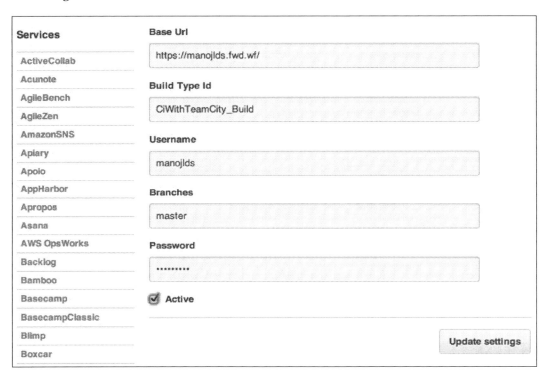

The **Base Url** is the URL of the TeamCity server. Note that the TeamCity server has to be accessible to GitHub, and hence must be a public link.

 Base Url specified in the previous screenshot, `http://manojlds.fwd.wf/`, is the forwarded link to the TeamCity server instance running on my workstation. The forwarding, in this case, was provided by `https://forwardhq.com/` and was used to test out the hook integration.

The **Build Type Id** is the internal TeamCity ID of the build configuration that needs to be triggered. We also need to provide the **Username** and **Password** to authenticate against the TeamCity server.

Branches can be specified to only trigger on changes to a particular branch, say, master.

Clicking on **Update settings** saves the settings. We will now have a **Test Hook** button available, which can be used to verify that the hook works as expected. Once this is configured, pushes to the master branch on the repo will automatically trigger the build configuration with the ID `CiWithTeamCity_Build`.

This method of using a hook on GitHub can be useful to reduce the need for our TeamCity server to poll repositories to detect changes. This is especially needed when the TeamCity server has a lot of VCS roots to be polled, since it reduces the load on the server by reducing the amount of polling that the server has to do. The hook also ensures that builds are triggered much more instantaneously than through polling, which is only done periodically.

 The biggest disadvantage of this method is that the TeamCity server has to be exposed to the internet (often through a reverse proxy.) This might not be ideal in many situations, and polling is the best option in those cases.

Using the TeamCity.GitHub plugin

The `TeamCity.GitHub` plugin (`https://github.com/jonnyzzz/TeamCity.GitHub`) adds build status integration between TeamCity and GitHub. The plugin adds the ability to view the status of the builds for particular commits and even pull requests.

Once the plugin is installed, it provides a new **Build Feature**, named **Report change status to GitHub**. Let's add this build feature to the build configuration named `build` in the `CI with TeamCity` project created in *Chapter 3, Getting Your CI Up and Running*. The settings that need to be configured for this build feature are shown in the following screenshot:

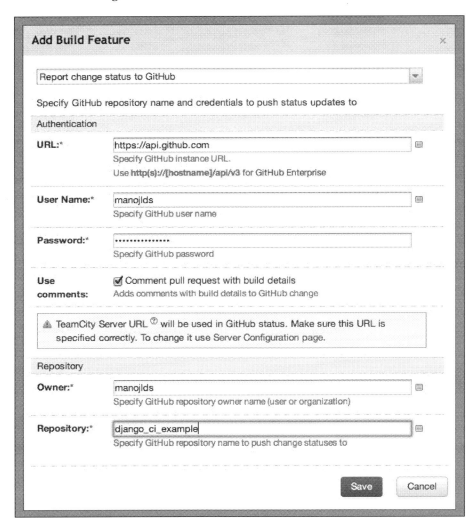

The **URL** field is used to specify the GitHub API URL. This can be left to the default value of `https://api.github.com` for repositories hosted on GitHub. It can be changed appropriately if GitHub Enterprise is used. Authentication details are provided using the **User Name** and **Password** fields.

The **Comment pull request with build details** option can be enabled to provide information regarding the status of the build in the corresponding commit or pull request in the form of comments.

Under the **Repository** section, the **Owner** and **Repository** fields are used to provide the user/organization name and the name of the repository itself.

Let's **Save** the build feature to add it to the build configuration.

Now, for new builds for commits on GitHub, the plugin automatically adds comments on the commit's page, indicating the status of the build, as shown in the following screenshot:

As can be seen in the screenshot, the comments (one to start a new build and another for success) are added using the credentials that we added in the build feature.

 The commit with the build status comments can be accessed at
`https://github.com/manojlds/django_ci_example/`
`commit/fcd5c5d5db3d35aa3c7b51586bb9b44137ed8add.`

Support for pull requests

Pull requests, mentioned in passing in previous sections, are one of the primary ways that users collaborate on projects in GitHub. The typical GitHub workflow to make a contribution to a project is to fork the project, make the necessary changes in the forked version, and send back a pull request to the original project, thereby asking the owner to accept the changes. This workflow is mainly applicable to open source projects, where contributors outside the core group are encouraged to send pull requests for any desired changes.

As the owner of a repository, we may want to also build the pull requests so that the status of the build can be used as a factor when accepting the pull request. It is already possible to build the pull requests for a repository using TeamCity.

Let's set up pull request building for the `django_ci_example` project. In the **VCS root** settings for the project, we can add the following to the branch specification:

```
+:refs/pull/*/merge
```

This makes TeamCity look at the pull requests that are added through GitHub.

Now, when a pull request is issued on the repository, the pull request is automatically built on TeamCity, and the status of the build is shown in the pull request page, as shown in the following screenshot:

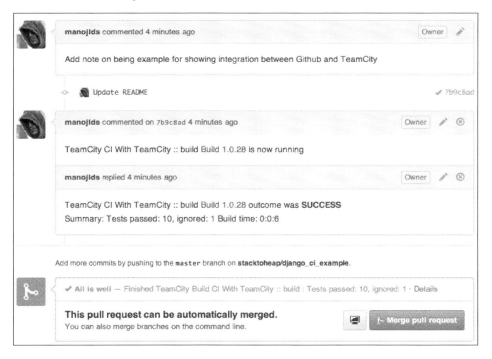

The most important information here is at the bottom of the screenshot, where we see GitHub proclaim that things are fine with the pull request from the build point of view as well, since the build has passed on TeamCity.

Since we enabled the comment option, the comments regarding starting a build and its success were added as well.

 The pull request used in this example can be accessed at `https://github.com/manojlds/django_ci_example/pull/1`.

Pull requests configured to automatically build on TeamCity need to be used carefully, especially in the case of open source projects, as it enables any person to execute code on our build servers just by submitting pull requests.

Integrating with GitHub issue tracker

Integration with the GitHub issue tracker can be obtained through the use of the `GitHub-issue` plugin (`https://github.com/milgner/TeamCityGithub`)

Once the plugin is installed, **GitHubIssues** must be available as an **Issue Tracker** from the **Administration | Issue Tracker** section. The settings to be configured to add the issue tracker are shown in the following screenshot:

We choose **GitHubIssues** as the **Connection Type**. The display name is given as `GitHub` but can be any name that makes sense.

The repository is given the name `manojlds/django_ci_example`, which is the fully qualified name of the repository under consideration.

Again, authentication details are passed through the **Username** and **Password** fields.

The **Ticket Pattern** is the most important setting. It is used to set the **regular expression (regex)** that will be applied against commit messages to link the commits with the corresponding issues.

Generally, a commit message follows some pattern to associate the issue/bug report/story number. For example `"#1 Fixing README"` could be a commit that was done to address the issue #1. The regex `#(\d+)` is used to extract the issue number from such a message.

Once the issue tracker connection is created, the **Changes** details for builds will start to provide links to the issue on the issue tracker (in this GitHub, issues for the repository), as shown in the following screenshot:

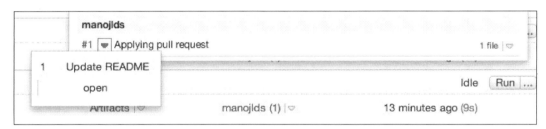

In the previous screenshot, the build had run for the change `#1 Applying pull request`. The `#1` value is automatically converted into a link to the issue #1, `http://github.com/manojlds/django_ci_example/issues/1`. On hovering over the down arrow, we also get a preview of the issue: its title (**Update README**) and also the status (**open**).

Additionally, the issues information is populated in the **Issues** tab of the particular build and also in the **Issue Log** tab of the build configuration.

The plugin for GitHub issues is not designed to work with multiple repositories at the moment. It is, hence, not usable when a single TeamCity is used to build projects from multiple repositories.

 Out of the box, TeamCity has support for YouTrack, JIRA, and Bugzilla issue trackers. The integration is pretty similar to that with GitHub issues obtained through the use of a plugin. Integrations with these issues, issue trackers can also be enabled from **Administration | Integrations | Issue Tracker**.

Build monitors

Build monitors are an essential part of any CI setup. Build monitors provide at-a-glance visibility on the status of the builds that concern a team. They are generally positioned such that any team member can quickly know the status of the builds while doing their work.

Such tools to provide information on the status of the builds are in line with one of the important practices of CI, as mentioned in *Chapter 1, Introduction*, providing visibility on what's happening with the builds.

 Generally, build monitors are set up with a display (TV/monitor) that shows them in fullscreen. The display is connected to a computer that has the client/browser needed for the build monitor. These days, small computers such as the Raspberry Pi are used to drive build monitors rather than desktops/laptops.

There are many plugins and tools that can be used as build monitors when using TeamCity as the CI tool. Some of these are discussed in this section.

Team Piazza

Team Piazza (`https://github.com/timomeinen/team-piazza`) is a plugin for TeamCity and is currently my favorite build monitor. Team Piazza adds a **Team Piazza Build Monitor** link for every project and build. Being a plugin to TeamCity, it doesn't need any external application/client to display the build monitor.

> The **enable status widget** option in the **General Settings** page of a build configuration has to be checked for Team Piazza (and many other plugins) to get the status information of the build configuration. When we created the first build configuration in *Chapter 3, Getting your CI Up and Running*, we enabled the same, citing build monitors as an example of a use case that needed it to be enabled.

The page shows the build status of the project or the build configuration clearly, with the background of the entire page being green on success and red on failure. The Team Piazza build monitor page also shows the authors/committers for the project, the build numbers, and even projects that are being built. The following screenshot shows the Team Piazza build monitor page for the Java CI with TeamCity project we created in *Chapter 4, TeamCity for Java Projects*:

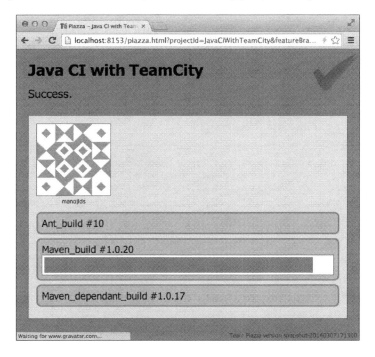

The green background clearly indicates that the project is in a success state (all the build configurations are passing.) We can also see that the build numbered 1.0.20 of maven_build build configuration is currently building.

The following screenshot shows the `CI with TeamCity` project, created in *Chapter 3*, *Getting Your CI Up and Running*, with the `Functional Tests` build configuration failing:

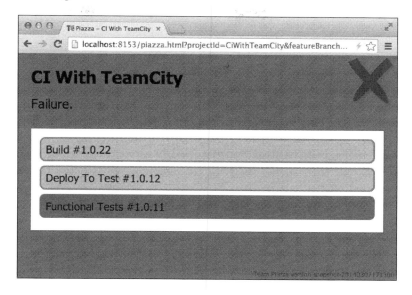

 Team Piazza also comes with a settings page that can be accessed from **Administration | Piazza Notifier**. The settings page is minimalistic at the moment, and only controls whether user pictures should be shown only on failures or always.

Project Monitor

Project Monitor (`https://github.com/pivotal/projectmonitor`) is a Rails application that can display the status of multiple projects in a single page. It has support for multiple CI servers, including TeamCity.

Project Monitor supports both push (webhooks) and pull (polling) methods to get the build status information. Polling should work out of the box on Teamcity, but webhooks requires the `TcWebhooks` plugin (`http://sourceforge.net/apps/trac/tcplugins/wiki/TcWebHooks`) to be installed in the TeamCity server.

Webhooks is the preferred approach as the TeamCity server can push information to Project Monitor only when the status changes, rather than have Project Monitor poll the server constantly, thereby increasing the load both on Project Monitor itself and TeamCity as well.

Upon creating a project on Project Monitor and choosing Webhooks as the desired method, a webhooks URL is provided. This URL is to be used by TeamCity to provide the updated information about builds to Project Monitor.

Once the `TcWebhooks` plugin is installed, it needs to be configured for the projects that need to be displayed on Project Monitor. It can be configured from the **WebHooks** tab of a project. The dialog to add a webhook for the `CI With TeamCity` project is shown in the following screenshot:

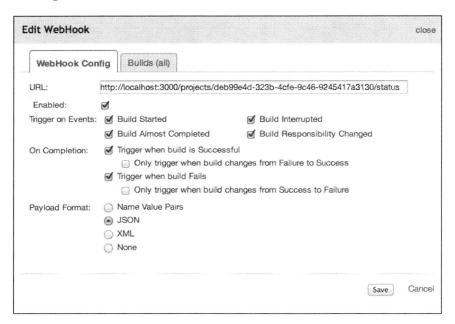

The **URL** field is to be filled with the WebHook URL provided from Project Monitor. Here we have enabled triggers for all events. The **Payload Format** needs to be **JSON** for it to be compatible with Project Monitor.

A sample Project Monitor screen, configured for two projects, is shown in the following screenshot:

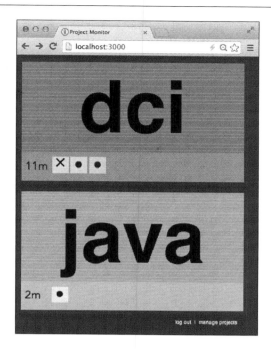

Build lights

Build lights are allied tools to build monitors. Build lights give information about the status of the build through (innovative) usage of lights — LEDs, lava lamps, and so on. Many teams use only build lights to convey the build status, while others use both build monitors and build lights.

 Build lights add an extra bit of fun to the entire process, with lots of innovations around how the build lights are constructed and used.

TeamFlash (`https://github.com/Readify/TeamFlash`) is a plugin that adds support for Delcom USB lights (`http://www.delcomproducts.com/products_ usblmp.asp`) to TeamCity.

Notifications

We have already seen build status notifications through IDE integrations. Notifications can also be configured to be sent through e-mail, Jabber, and also by using the Windows Tray Notifier. There are also a number of plugins to add support to send notifications through other mediums (such as Twitter).

The following screenshot shows the Quick View window of the Windows Tray Notifier:

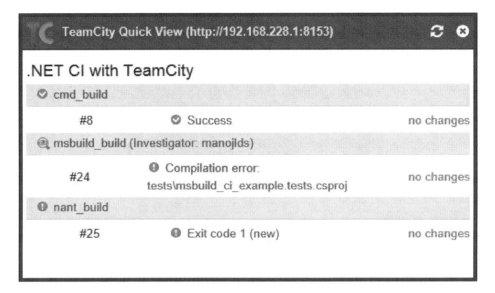

 There are also TeamCity apps for iOS, Android, and Windows Phone that can be used to get a quick view on the build status even on the move (use sparingly, however).

Summary

In this chapter, we looked at how TeamCity provides integrations with various different tools with the aim of making CI and interacting with TeamCity a seamless experience.

Through built-in features, a variety of plugins, and also support from third-party tools and service providers, TeamCity can work well with a lot of tools.

IDE integrations enable developers to work with TeamCity without ever having to leave the comfort of their IDEs. Integrations with providers such as GitHub enable richer use of features provided by both TeamCity and the provider and builds upon their synergy. Such integrations may not be always necessary, but they do provide remarkable improvements over the default setup. For example, we can live with polling a GitHub repository, rather than configuring hooks as described in this chapter. They sure do make the VCS change trigger process much more efficient and instantaneous.

In the next chapter, we will be looking at how team members can use TeamCity as a collaborative CI tool.

9
TeamCity for a Member of the Team

In this chapter, we will take a look at how a user of TeamCity can take advantage of the features provided by the web interface of TeamCity to achieve various tasks that are expected of them in a Continuous Integration setup.

Such tasks would include communicating build failures with other team members, navigating across projects of interests, searching historical build data, and so on.

Managing projects of interest

In an organization, a single TeamCity server might be used to host CI for multiple project teams. Hence, there might be TeamCity projects that are not of any particular interest to a team member. Depending on the team structure and setup of TeamCity, even certain build configurations may not be of interest to all the users of a TeamCity server.

TeamCity provides the ability to hide the web interface, projects, and build configurations that may not be of interest to a particular user. Projects and build configurations can also be reordered as desired.

 Administrators can use TeamCity's **Authentication** and **Roles** settings to have projects accessible to only a set of concerned users. The ability to hide/show projects discussed here is about user preferences and not about access control.

Hiding projects

Projects can be hidden, unhidden, and reordered using the **Configure Visible Projects** link found at the top-right corner of the **Overview** page, just below the navigation bar. Clicking on this link brings up the dialog shown in the following screenshot:

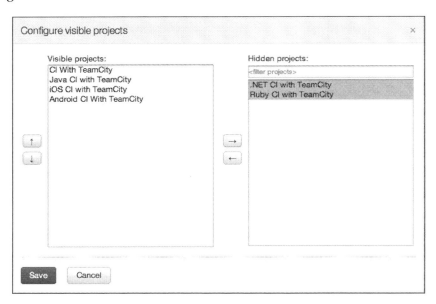

In this screenshot, two projects are hidden and the others are visible. Using the left and right arrows, one or more projects can be hidden or made visible. The up and down arrows can be used to reorder the visible projects so that projects of utmost interest can always be at the top of the web interface.

 It is also possible to hide projects by clicking on **x** to the right of the project title in the **Overview** page.

Hiding build configurations

Build configurations can be hidden by clicking on the down arrow next to the **no hidden** text, towards the right of a project in the **Overview** page. The pop-up menu has the **Hide, show or reorder build configurations...** link to get the dialog to show, hide, and reorder build configurations within the project concerned, as shown in the following screenshot:

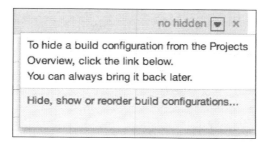

The **Configure visible build configurations** dialog is similar to that of the projects.

When build configurations are hidden, the **no hidden** text, obviously, changes to show the number of hidden build configurations in the project. The pop-up menu shows all the hidden build configurations. These build configurations can also be unhidden directly from the pop-up menu by clicking on the **show** link, as shown in the following screenshot:

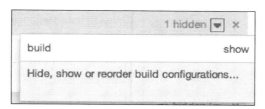

Navigating across projects

From any page of TeamCity, it is very easy to navigate to any project/build configuration page. Clicking on the *P* key on the keyboard brings up the **Projects** pop-up menu, as shown in the following screenshot:

The same menu, of course, can also be brought up by clicking/ hovering on the down arrow next to the **Projects** link in the navigation bar.

With the context in the **<filter projects and build configurations>** textbox, it is now possible to type a few characters of a project or build configuration that we want to navigate to. This will filter the list to show only the matching projects and build configurations, which can then be selected by using arrow keys and navigated to by hitting return. The following screenshot shows the list of **Projects** filtered for the `fun` search term:

 This workflow enables us to quickly navigate to the concerned projects and build configurations only by using the keyboard. Of course, all this is possible with the mouse as well, but as any power user knows, the keyboard is the fastest route.

Investigating investigations

We have already mentioned investigations in passing in *Chapter 8, Integration with Other Tools*. In this section, we will look at it in more detail and understand the purpose better.

Investigations are the mechanism through which a member of the team can inform others that they are looking into the build issues in one or more build configurations.

 Investigations are not only assigned for build configurations, but can also be assigned to one or more failed tests and other problems in a build configuration as well.

A team member can also assign another team member to investigate the problems in a build based on the VCS changes shown in TeamCity.

Assigning investigations

Assigning investigations to oneself, or any other team member, is straightforward. This can be done by hovering over the down arrow next to the concerned build configuration and choosing **Investigate...** from the menu. This brings up a dialog similar to the one shown in the following screenshot:

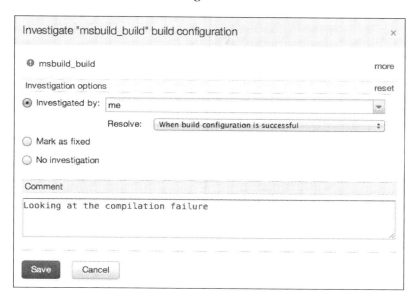

As can be seen from the screenshot, the dialog was opened to investigate a failure on the `msbuild_build` build configuration. Clicking on the **more** link shows other failing build configurations in the same project, thereby enabling us to assign investigations for multiple build configurations.

Under **Investigation options**, the **Investigated by** field provides the ability to choose **me** (self) or another team member as the investigator of the failure.

The **Resolve** field has two options that can be chosen:

- **Manually**: With this, the investigation will be manually set as resolved by a team member
- **When build configuration is successful**: With this, the investigation will be automatically set as resolved by TeamCity when the build configuration(s) pass

The **Manually** option might be used when the build configuration has been failing randomly. The investigation can itself be about the randomness and hence a successful run need not indicate that the root problem has actually been solved.

Comment can be used to pass an extra bit of information about the investigation so that others looking at the investigation can understand what is being done.

Clicking on **Save** will add the investigation and let others know that the build failure is being looked at.

> The **Mark as Fixed** option is used to mark an ongoing investigation as fixed/resolved. The **No Investigation** option is used to clear a set investigation.

When an investigation is set to a user, the **You are assigned to investigate the build configuration** notice is visible to them. Clicking on this link shows information about the investigation, including options to fix or reassign the investigation, as shown in the following screenshot:

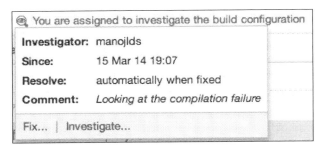

Clicking on **Fix...** will bring up the same investigation dialog with the **Mark as Fixed** option selected.

> Investigations can be assigned for tests by navigating to the concerned test and choosing the **Investigate/Mute...** link from the menu that comes up when you hover over the down arrow.

Viewing active investigations

It is possible to view all the investigations assigned to us by clicking on the number that appears before the username in the navigation bar.

> As can be easily deduced, the number next to the username shows the number of active investigations. The number is highlighted if any new investigations are assigned to us; nothing is shown if there are no assigned investigations.

This brings us to the **My Investigations** page, which shows the list of active investigations assigned to us, with options to fix, reassign, or remove them. An example of a listing of active investigations on this page is shown in the following screenshot:

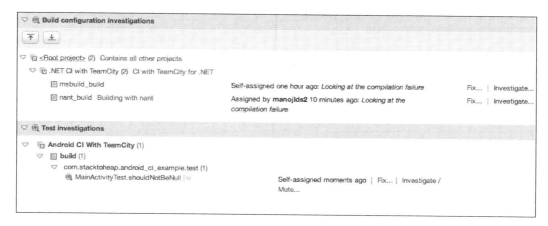

The investigations are grouped into **Build configuration investigations** and **Test investigations**.

Managing current and muted problems

The **Current problems** tab of a project shows the issues across the build configurations of the project. This tab can be used to peruse all problems such as test failures, build failures, non-zero exits, and so on.

The **Muted problems** tab shows the problems that have been ignored in build configurations.

Only project-level or the entire server-level administrators, or those assigned with the mute permission, can mute problems.

Tests and other problems can be muted such that their continued failures do not affect the outcome of the build configurations concerned.

Problems can be muted when, for example, an integration test fails due to a known temporary issue in an external service. The concerned tests may be muted so that the builds are not halted while the external service is facing the issue.

Build problems/test failures can be muted by using the **Investigate/Mute...** link in the pop-up menu that appears when you hover over the respective down arrow.

 As previously mentioned, muting problems and tests is only possible for administrators or those with the mute permission. Hence, the **Investigate/Mute...** link won't be available for other team members; only the **Investigate...** link will be available.

The **Investigate/Mute** dialog is shown in the following screenshot:

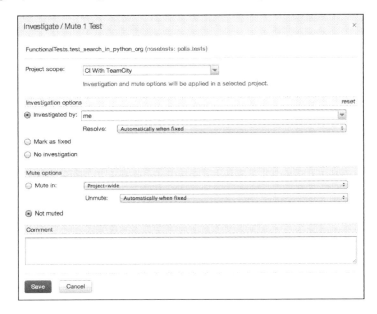

The investigation options are similar to the **Investigate** dialog we saw previously. Under **Mute Options**, the **Mute in** field is used to set whether the problem needs to be muted in the entire project or only in the specific build configuration.

The **Unmute** field has the following options that determine when the problems/tests are to be unmuted:

- **Automatically when fixed**: The problems/tests are unmuted when they get fixed or the test is passed.

- **Manually**: The problems/tests are unmuted manually using the **Not muted** option.

- **On a specific date**: We can specify when to unmute problems/tests on a particular date. This can be the date when the problem is expected to automatically resolve itself.

- **Comment**: Comments can be added to give information about the investigation or reasons for muting.

TeamCity universal search

TeamCity comes with a universal search feature to search for builds, using various attributes such as changes, tests, status, build number, and so on. This is a really useful feature, especially to find historical information about a project that has been running for a long time.

A universal search can be performed using the **Search** textbox at the extreme right-hand side of the navigation bar.

> TeamCity uses a syntax for the search that is similar to the Lucene query syntax.
>
> Apache Lucene is an indexing and search library. Popular search servers such as Solr and Elastic Search make use of Lucene.

For example, to find all the builds for build configurations that had `build` in their names and also included the `.gitignore` file in their changes, we can use the following query:

```
files:(.gitignore) configuration:(build)
```

The `files` and `configuration` parameters are the search fields, and they get `.gitignore` and `build` as the values, respectively. The results are shown in a preview pop up, as shown in the following screenshot:

Clicking on *Shift + Enter* takes us to the dedicated search page (seen in the next screenshot).

As another example, to find all the builds that had a change with `fixing` as the commit message, we can use the search term `changes:(fixing)`. A sample set of results for such a search is shown in the following screenshot:

As can be seen from the screenshot, the builds listed have the change **Fixing flake8 issues**, hence this is why they match the search term.

Actions on build configurations

A team member can perform multiple actions on a build configuration using the **Actions** button at the top-right corner of a build configuration's page. These actions are described in this section.

Pausing triggers in a build configuration

Many a time, the settings of a build configuration might be undergoing a change. It might be failing, resulting in the need to prevent further builds from being configured to investigate this change properly. For such reasons, TeamCity provides the ability to pause a build configuration for a while until the issue is resolved.

The **Pause triggers in this configuration...** action is used to pause a build temporarily so that no automatic triggers can trigger a run of the build. The build configurations can, of course, still be triggered manually. The following screenshot shows the **Pause** build configuration dialog:

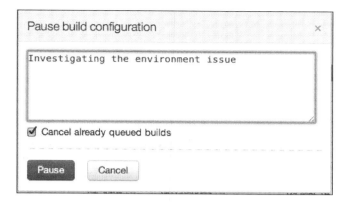

This dialog provides the ability to add a message that describes why the build configuration is being paused. The **Cancel already queued builds** option can be checked to remove builds that are waiting in the queue as well.

This adds the notice, shown in the following screenshot, to the build configuration page:

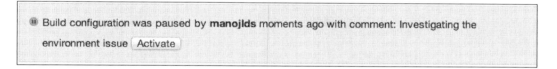

The **Activate** button can be used to activate the build configuration again.

Checking for pending changes

TeamCity polls the VCS root for changes in a periodic interval. If we know that a change has been pushed to the repository and TeamCity has not yet detected it, we can use the **Check for pending changes** action to force TeamCity to collect the changes for the concerned build configuration.

Enforcing clean checkout

The **Enforce clean checkout...** action can be used to clean the working directory in one or more agents that are running the build configuration.

We might need to clean the checkout directory if we know that some external action has changed the contents of the directory. For example, we may have altered some files while investigating a build failure on the agent and hence want to clear those changes.

Clicking on this action brings up the **Enforce clean checkout on agents** dialog, which is shown in the following screenshot:

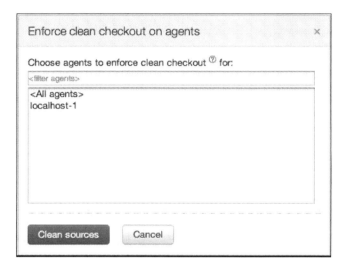

This dialog provides the option to choose one or more agents where the working directory for the build configuration must be cleared. Clicking on **Clean sources** ensures that the clean up happens on the next run of the build configuration.

Perusing the build logs of the build configuration on its next run shows that the working directory is cleaned and a fresh checkout is done:

```
Updating sources: server side checkout

[22:13:05][Updating sources] Using vcs information from agent file:
97adbabe47870895.xml

[22:13:05][Updating sources] Will perform clean checkout. Reason: Clean
checkout requested by user

[22:13:05][Updating sources] Building and caching clean patch for VCS
root: rails_github

[22:13:05][Updating sources] Transferring cached clean patch for VCS
root: rails_github

[22:13:05][Updating sources] Repository sources transferred: 37.34 KB
total
```

There are multiple other ways to enforce a clean checkout. One way that we have already seen is setting up the **Clean all files in the checkout directory before the build** option in the **VCS settings** of a build configuration. This ensures that the cleanup automatically happens for every build.

Another route is to go through the agent. From an agent's page, we can click on **Clean sources on this agent** to bring up the **Choose build configurations** dialog from where we can choose the build configurations whose checkout directory must be cleared.

Yet another way to enforce a clean checkout is to use the **Run Custom Build** option (done by clicking on the ellipses next to the **Run** button). One of the options in the custom build dialog is **clean all files in the checkout directory before the build**.

On top of these explicit settings, TeamCity also cleans the checkout directory due to other reasons such as changing of VCS root, running out of disk space, and so on.

Summary

In this chapter, we looked at how TeamCity makes it easy for team members to do the following:

- Focus on the projects they are working on
- Navigate across projects and build configurations efficiently
- Peruse problems and take steps to solve them
- Communicate with other team members regarding failures and what steps are being taken to fix them
- Search for builds, old and new, using various attributes such as build number, change message, files changed, and so on

TeamCity comes across as a CI platform where members of a team can collaborate, communicate, take ownership of and fix issues, and hence practice some of the best practices of CI.

In the next chapter, we will look at some of the more advanced features of TeamCity such as templates and Meta-Runners.

10
Taking It a Level Up

In this chapter, we will be looking at some of the more advanced concepts in TeamCity. These concepts can improve the entire setup of TeamCity and aid in moving towards a better CI setup.

While many of these concepts need not be implemented or used in a TeamCity server, their usage definitely takes the CI setup up a level.

We will be covering the following advanced topics in this chapter:

- Build configuration templates
- Meta-Runners
- Tagging and pinning builds
- Build history and artifacts cleanup
- Build queue priorities
- Build script interaction with TeamCity

Build configuration templates

Templates allow us to create similar build configurations easily, without having to duplicate the similar configurations between them. Templates in TeamCity are entities from which build configurations can be created. Also, build configurations can be based on templates. Such build configurations inherit all the configurations from the template that they are associated with.

As is obvious, templates are very useful when we need to have multiple build configurations that are all very similar. Instead of creating individual build configurations that have these similar configurations repeated, we could have these similarities in a template and have each build configuration with only its minor differences.

TeamCity also has the ability to copy an existing build configuration and create a new one. This feature can be used when creating a one-off similar build. When we need to create multiple similar configurations, the copy method must be avoided.

The advantage of having the similarities in a template is that any change to the configurations in a template is automatically propagated to all the associated templates. If, instead, build configurations were created individually, we would have to perform the change (as minor as it might have been) on each build configuration.

 A good example of build configurations leveraging template features is that of the ones used to deploy an application. Each environment can have a build configuration to deploy the application, such as `deploy-to-test`, `deploy-to-uat`, `deploy-to-prod`, and so on. Obviously, all these build configurations that ought to perform the same set of build steps probably have the same VCS settings and the same dependencies. Usually, the environment to deploy to is passed as an argument to a deployment script or set as a system environment variable. This is usually the only difference across the build configurations.

In such a scenario, a template can be used to define all the configurations needed to do a deployment, and the individual build configurations that are based on the template can override the build parameters alone as needed.

There are two ways to create a template:

- Create a template from the administration page of a project, much like how build configurations are created
- Extract a template from an existing build configuration

 The latter is probably the more common approach. We would generally create a build configuration, and when we see that we need other similar build configurations, we extract a template from the existing one.

It should also be noted that when a template is extracted from a build configuration, the build configuration is also associated with the template.

We will look at these two ways of creating templates and put them to effective use in the next sections.

Creating templates from scratch

We can create new templates from scratch much like how we create build configurations. For this, we click on the **Create template** button under the **Build Configuration Templates** section of a project's administration page, which is shown in the following screenshot:

The next steps are exactly the same as those to create a build configuration—provide a name and other **General settings**, attach **VCS Roots**, add **Build steps**, and so on. We can save the build template and see it listed in the **Build Configuration Templates** section of the project.

The build configurations associated with a template get all the settings from the template, and most of these cannot be edited/overridden in the build configurations.

Any setting that needs to be overridden in the build configurations must be defined using parameters. The general idea is that a template uses build parameters in sections that it expects to be overridden/defined in the build configurations. The build parameters can be either unset, in which case the build configurations have to define them, or provided with default values.

For example, if we want to allow the build configurations to potentially have their own build number formats, we can specify the **Build number** format in the **General Settings** section as `%build.format%`. From the **Build parameters** section, we can provide the `1.0.%build.counter%` value for the `%build.format%` parameter, or even let it be undefined, so that the build configurations can either override/edit this value.

Similarly, for a build step, if the command to be run is `deploy.sh <environment_name>`, we can define the command-line runner to run `deploy.sh %environment%`. The `%environment%` parameter can be unset in the template so that every build configuration that is created out of the template can define it.

Moreover, the parameters needed for templates within a project can come from project parameters too, ensuring that build configurations in a project share the same settings.

The **Configuration Parameters** defined for the template are shown in the following screenshot:

Configuration Parameters ⑦			
Name	**Value**		
build.format	%MAJOR_MINOR%%build.counter%	edit	delete
environment	<value is required>	edit	undeletable
MAJOR_MINOR *(inherited from project "CI With TeamCity")*	1.0.	edit	undeletable

> In the screenshot, **MAJOR_MINOR** is a parameter inherited from the project, as was defined in *Chapter 3, Getting Your CI Up and Running*, for the CI with TeamCity project. We have reused this parameter in the `%build.format%` parameter value.

Creating build configurations from the template

There are two ways to create a build configuration from a template. From the administration page of a project, we can click on the **Create from template** button under the **Build Configurations** section, which is shown in the following screenshot:

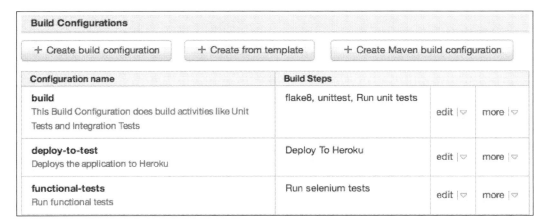

Alternatively, we can navigate to a template's page and click on the **Create Build Configuration** button present in the right-hand side bar, which is shown in the following screenshot:

Using either method brings up the **Create Build Configuration From Template** dialog where we can populate the necessary information to create a build configuration from the template. The dialog is shown in the following screenshot:

As can be seen from the screenshot, the dialog also provides us with the ability to change or provide values for the build parameters. This makes it very easy for us to know the build parameters involved and their default values, and also to edit/override them while creating the build configuration.

Clicking on **Create** creates the build configuration based on the template.

Creating templates from existing build configurations

The other way to create a template is from existing build configurations. From a build configuration's configuration page, we can click on the **Extract Template** button in the right-hand side bar, as shown in the following screenshot:

 The previous screenshot also features the **Associate with Template** button. This can be used to associate an existing build configuration to an existing template. When doing so, the settings that come from the template take precedence over the ones already configured in the build configuration.

This brings up the **Extract Template** dialog as shown in the following screenshot:

Clicking on **Extract** creates the new template. The build configuration is also automatically attached to the template.

> When a build configuration is associated with a template, many of the settings such as the name, description, and so on, that are obviously specific to a build configuration are editable. Most other settings inherited from the template cannot be edited.
>
> In most cases where a setting is a collection of items, more items can be added, but items from the template cannot be removed. For example, new VCS roots can be added, but the ones from the template cannot be detached. Similarly, additional build steps can be added, but the ones from the template cannot be edited or removed.

Going meta with Meta-Runners

We have seen that build runners can be very handy. Even though most build runners can be replaced with an equivalent command using the command-line runner, build runners come with the convenience of easily setting up build steps, along with the necessary agent requirements and parameters.

Meta-Runners provide a straightforward way to create custom build runners. Meta-Runners can be thought of as a way to avoid duplications in build steps across build configurations.

> While templates can be used to create and maintain build configurations that are very similar, Meta-Runners can be used across build configurations that perform the same build steps. Moreover, a build configuration can only be based on one template, but it can make use of multiple Meta-Runners.

In *Chapter 3, Getting Your CI Up and Running*, we created the `deploy-to-test` build configuration that deploys the Django application to Heroku. Using this build configuration as an example, we can see how we can extract a Meta-Runner `Deploy To Heroku` that can be used by any build configuration that wants to deploy to Heroku.

Recall that the `deploy-to-test` build configuration had a simple command-line runner that executed the following commands:

```
git remote add heroku git@heroku.com:django-ci-example.git
git push heroku master
```

To create a generic Meta-Runner out of this, we need to provide a way to push to any remote, rather than just `git@heroku.com:django-ci-example.git`.

 Deploying to Heroku using remotes needs the `ssh` keys to be set up on the agent. The example used here just illustrates Meta-Runners and may not be ideal for production use.

As mentioned in *Chapter 6, TeamCity for Ruby Projects*, we can use a gem such as `heroku-headless` (`https://github.com/moredip/heroku-headless`).

As expected, we will do this by extracting the remote out into a build parameter. The command-line runner will have the following as the **Custom Script** to be run:

```
git remote add heroku %heroku.remote%
git push heroku master
```

We will provide the value for the `%heroku.remote%` parameter in the **Build Parameters** section of the build configuration.

Now we are ready to create a Meta-Runner from this build configuration. This can be done by clicking on the **Extract Meta-Runner** button in the right-hand side bar of the build configuration settings page. This brings up the **Extract Meta-Runner** dialog, which is shown in the following screenshot:

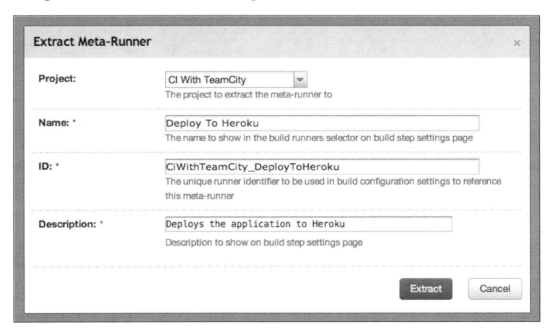

In the dialog, we give a name to the Meta-Runner. This is the name that will appear in the **Runner Type** field when configuring a build step for a build configuration.

Click on **Extract** to create the Meta-Runner. Once the Meta-Runner is created, we can see it listed in the **Meta-Runners** tab on the project administration page. We can also edit the Meta-Runner to fine-tune it as desired.

> A Meta-Runner is essentially an XML configuration (much like most TeamCity configurations) that can be edited directly from the web interface.

The following screenshot shows the edit page of the `Deploy To Heroku` Meta-Runner that we just created:

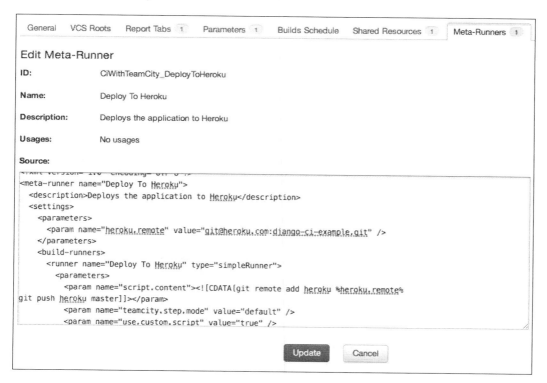

The Meta-Runner extracts all the parameters and steps defined in the build configuration. We can edit the Meta-Runner to have only the necessary parameters and steps.

Using Meta-Runners

We can now use the Meta-Runner that we created pretty much like a normal build runner. We will remove the existing build step in the `deploy-to-test` build configuration (from which we extracted the Meta-Runner) and add a `Deploy To Heroku` Meta-Runner-based build step.

 We can also disable build steps if we don't want to remove them while experimenting.

In the **New Build Step** page, for the **Runner type** field, the newly created **Deploy To Heroku** Meta-Runner is available, as shown in the following screenshot:

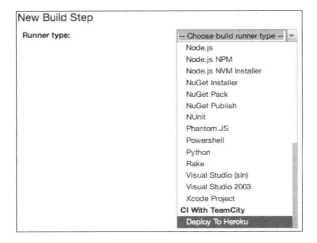

Once we choose the `Deploy To Heroku` Meta-Runner, we can see that the `heroku.remote` parameter is one of the fields to be configured. Since we created the Meta-Runner with the `heroku.remote` parameter with the value `git@heroku.com:django-ci-example.git`, that remote is available by default. The `Deploy To Heroku` runner configuration page is shown in the following screenshot:

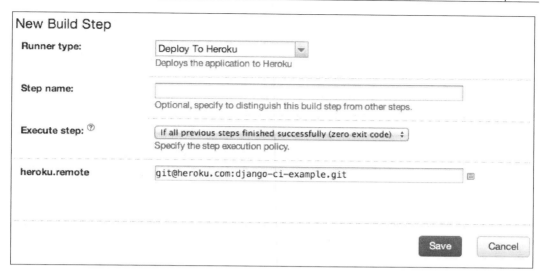

 It is possible to remove the value for parameters in the Meta-Runner XML so that no default values are present for the fields.

We can click on **Save** to add the build step. The new build step, based on the `Deploy To Heroku` Meta-Runner, will function in the same way as the previous build step based on the command-line runner.

 Of course, the value of Meta-Runners becomes more apparent when we create them out of multiple build steps. The same set of steps that may be repeated across multiple configurations can be extracted into Meta-Runners.

Build result actions

In *Chapter 9, TeamCity for a Member of the Team*, we had a look at **Actions** on build configurations. There are also actions that can be performed on build configuration results, as shown in the following screenshot:

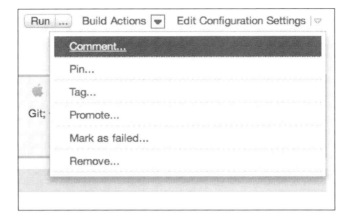

These actions and their use cases are discussed in this section.

Commenting on build results

The **Comment...** build action is used to allow users to communicate extra information about a particular build to other team members. Depending on the workflow, the comment could be about the changes included in the build, the bugs that are fixed, giving information that the build could be deployed to an environment, and so on.

Clicking on the **Comment...** link brings up the **Add build comment** dialog, which is shown in the following screenshot:

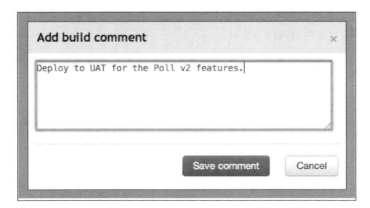

Clicking on **Save comment** adds the comment on the build result. The comment is shown in the build results page and is also available on the build configuration overview page where all the build results are listed, as shown in the following screenshot:

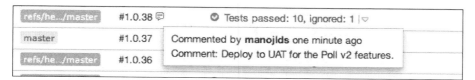

 The commenting feature is very simple, and any future comments only change the existing comment such that there is only one comment associated with a build result. This ensures that the necessary information is available without having to navigate through multiple comments.

Tagging build results

Tags can be added to build results to aid in filtering and searching. For example, if all the builds that are deployed to staging are marked with the staging tag, it becomes very easy to filter all the builds that are deployed to staging. Multiple tags can be added to a single build result and are delimited using a space, comma, or semicolon, as shown in the following screenshot:

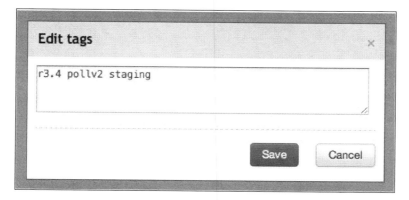

Once the tags are added, they can be used to filter and search for builds that match them. Tags are also listed in the **Overview** tab of the build configuration, where all the build results are listed.

 Tags can also be added/edited for a build result from the **Overview** tab of the build configuration by hovering over/clicking on the down arrow under the **Tags** column.

Pinning build results

Pinning is a way to mark build results that are never to be removed from the TeamCity server; the concept of pinning ties in with TeamCity's Artifact and Build History cleanup settings. Pinned builds are never cleaned up and will be maintained on the TeamCity server.

The **Pin Build** dialog is shown in the following screenshot:

As seen from the screenshot, we can provide a message/comment on why the build is being pinned. We can also edit the tags for the builds since tags are an allied concept to pinning.

 Usually, important builds, such as builds that are deployed to production, are pinned. So, apart from communicating to the TeamCity server that these builds should not be cleaned, pinned builds also quickly show important builds to team members as well.

Promoting builds

Promoting builds is a way to run a downstream build configuration using a different upstream build configuration (than the latest successful one) in a build chain.

For example, as seen in *Chapter 3, Getting Your CI Up and Running*, the build chain for the CI with TeamCity project is build -> deploy-to-test -> functional-tests.

If we trigger the deploy-to-test build by clicking on **Run**, it will use the latest build as the upstream build. However, if we wanted to run the deploy-to-test build for a different build, we can navigate to the particular build and use the **Promote** action. Clicking on the promote action brings up the **Promote Build** dialog, as shown in the following screenshot:

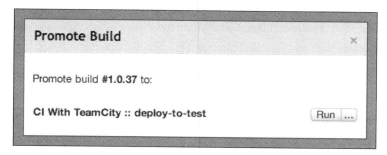

Clicking on **Run** will run the deploy-to-test build configuration with the upstream build as the chosen build rather than choosing the latest build.

Marking the build as successful or failed

This action, available only to project administrators and those with higher permissions or the ones with the **Change build status** permission, is used to manually mark a build as failed or successful.

There may be occasions when the fail or success state of a build may not be right and might have to be fixed manually. For example, a build might have passed due to issues with the build script not passing the correct exit code to TeamCity. In such cases, we can manually fix the status of the build (successful, in the example) as appropriate.

Usually, a wrongly passing build might have to be marked as failed. The other way around, marking a failing build as passed, should be used prudently as the risks associated with it are high. It might be better to actually fix the issue and get a passing build through the normal way.

Valid use cases for this include situations where (integration) tests are failing due to unavailability of external resources, and we want successful builds while the issue is being worked on.

Removing builds

The final action is the ability to remove a build result from the history of the build configuration. It can be used to manually clean up the build history, especially to remove old, failing builds.

The **Remove this build** dialog is shown in the following screenshot:

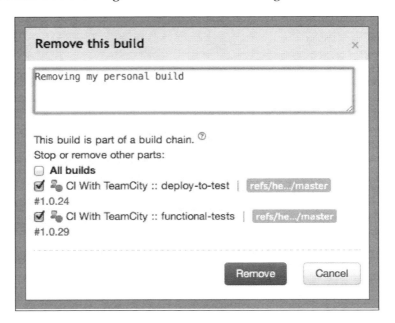

As can be seen from the screenshot, there is also the ability to remove the downstream builds in a build chain while removing an upstream build. In the screenshot, a personal build is being removed, which is one of the use cases for the **Remove** option.

This feature is available only to the administrators of the project or the server, or those with the **Remove finished build** permission. It must be used with caution and only when needed. Relying on the cleanup policies of the server to clean old builds might be a better option, if the removal is being done only to clear up history and old artifacts.

Removing old builds might be beneficial when a build configuration is being set up for the first time, and we want to remove the initial failures before we get the settings right. This helps to remove noise in the history of a build configuration.

Build history cleanup

As TeamCity continues to build our projects, the amount of disk space utilized by it keeps increasing. The artifacts, in particular, take up a lot of disk space. While disk space has become a lot cheaper these days, it is still not practical to let the disk usage keep increasing forever.

TeamCity has a very powerful cleanup feature that can be used to control how build history and artifacts are cleaned on the server. The cleanup is either run periodically or triggered manually. It can be configured for the server as a whole, while also overriding the settings, as needed, for individual projects and build configurations.

The **Build history clean-up** section can be reached from **Administration | Build history clean-up** (located in the left-hand side bar.) The following screenshot shows the settings page of this feature:

Clean-up settings ⓘ

Periodical clean-up: Enabled   [Disable]

Start time: [03 ⇕] h [00 ⇕] min
                        Next scheduled time: 24 Mar 14 03:00 GMT +0530

Stop clean-up if it takes   [   ] minutes
longer than: Leave blank if there is no limit for clean-up duration

                        [Save settings]

Start clean-up

Last time clean-up took: 1s [Start clean-up now]

Configure clean-up rules

Disk usage for all projects: free space: **120.98 GB**, total artifacts: **22.73 MB**, total logs: **3.92 MB**. View disk usage report

Manage clean-up rules for: [— Choose project — ⇕]

Under **Clean-up settings**, we can enable or disable **Periodical clean-up**. This is akin to running a cron job to clean up the history and artifacts at a particular time, specified by the **Start time** field.

 We would generally want **Start time** to be when the server is not used or moderately used, which would usually be some time in the night. The cleanup can potentially take a lot of server resources and can take a while, especially on servers with lots of builds, and hence it is prudent to avoid doing the cleanup during work hours.

The **Stop clean-up if it takes longer than** field is used to give a timeout for the cleanup process. This can used to ensure that the cleanup does not take a long time to complete. If the cleanup is not able to finish within this time, it is stopped, and the cleanup will resume at the next scheduled time.

The **Start clean-up now** button can be used to manually trigger a cleanup. This can be used when either the automatic cleanup is disabled, or we want to run a one-off cleanup process immediately.

The **Configure clean-up rules** section provides information on **disk usage** and also the ability to configure the rules for cleanup at the individual project level.

 The disk usage details provide information that can be used to make an informed choice as to which projects and build configurations need to be cleaned up with a more strict rule, and which need not.

The following section looks at the cleanup rules in detail.

Cleanup rules

By default, the cleanup rules, as defined for Root project, do not perform any cleanup, and the entire history and all the artifacts are kept forever. This default setting is inherited by all the projects. These settings can hence be changed at the root level or can be overridden for only the necessary projects (or even build configuration) depending on their disk usage.

A section of the table showing the cleanup rules for a project, in this case, Root project, and its children are shown in the following screenshot:

Configure clean-up rules

Disk usage for all projects: free space: **120.98 GB**, total artifacts: **22.73 MB**, total logs: **3.92 MB**. View disk usage report

Manage clean-up rules for: <Root project>

Project	Build configuration or template	What to clean-up	
		Light gray oblique text is used for inherited rules. Customised rules are in darker, regular font.	
<Root project> Contains all other projects Disk usage: 26.66 MB	<Default cleanup rules for all projects>	Everything is kept forever Do not prevent dependency artifacts cleanup	edit
.NET CI with TeamCity CI with TeamCity for .NET Disk usage: 2.13 MB	<Default cleanup rules for all configurations of this project and sub projects>	Everything is kept forever Do not prevent dependency artifacts cleanup	edit
	cmd_build Disk usage: <1 MB	Everything is kept forever Do not prevent dependency artifacts cleanup	edit
	msbuild_build Disk usage: <1 MB	Everything is kept forever Do not prevent dependency artifacts cleanup	edit
	nant_build Disk usage: 1.61 MB	Everything is kept forever Do not prevent dependency artifacts cleanup	edit
Android CI With TeamCity	<Default cleanup rules for all configurations of	Everything is kept forever	edit

The cleanup rules can be changed by clicking on the **edit** link next to the corresponding project or build configuration.

The cleanup rules can be configured to clean the build history, the artifacts, or everything.

> When the build history is cleaned, the statistical data for the build configuration is not cleared. This is a desirable behavior since we may want to be able to see (and use) the statistics of the build, but may not need the entire build run history. Only when we enable the rule to clean up everything is the statistical data cleaned up as well.

In addition, rules regarding the cleanup of dependencies can also be configured.

The following screenshot shows the **Edit clean-up rules for <Root project>** dialog, used to configure the cleanup rules for the Root project:

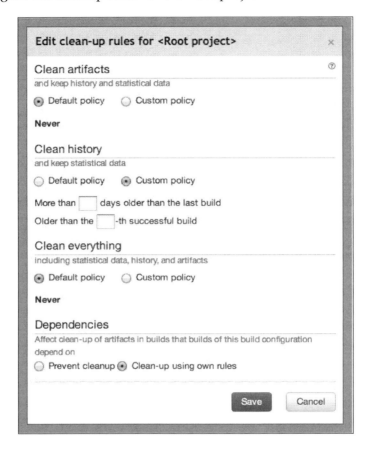

Leaving any of the settings as **Default Policy** makes it inherit the setting from the parent project. In case of the Root project, this will, of course, be the server default of not cleaning up anything.

In the screenshot, **Custom Policy** has been selected for the **Clean history** section. Here, we can see that we can configure the cleanup rules based on:

- **Days**: Build configuration history older than the given number of days is cleaned up
- **Number of builds**: Build configuration's history beyond the given number of builds since the latest is cleared

It is preferable to use the build number to clean up because the number of builds per day is not known. We generally want to keep the last, say, 100 builds (and the pinned builds), rather than the last 10 days' worth of builds. The latter could be 10 or 10,000 builds for all we know.

Archiving projects

While we are getting to know about cleaning up old builds and their artifacts, let's also look at a related activity—archiving projects that are not needed anymore.

As is the case with any project, there might come a time when the project is not in use anymore. The build configurations may just be idle since no one is working on the project. Even though the builds are idle, they still use up server resources, with VCS polling being one of the main resource hogs. The idle projects also come in the way in the **Overview** page and other places where projects are listed. This can be especially irksome when there are many such defunct projects (more specifically builds configured for old branches of a project).

Such projects can be archived. A project can be archived by clicking on the **Archive** button in the project's configuration page.

Once a project is archived, the build configurations within it are paused and do not run automatically anymore. They also stop polling for changes.

Configuring build priorities

The build queue in TeamCity, by default, ensures that builds are run in the order in which they came in (the classic **First In First Out** way).

 Build configurations in the queue can also be rearranged or even removed from the queue manually from the **Build Queue** page.

While this works for most cases, there are situations when we might need to ensure that certain build configurations are triggered as soon as possible. For example, build configurations that deploy to production definitely need to have agents assigned to them as soon as one becomes free.

At the other end of the spectrum, we can also have build configurations that may have low priority, and can be run only when other build configurations are not looking for agents. Build configurations running regression tests are examples of those that can have low priority. These tests can run for a long time, and it doesn't make sense to hold up other builds.

TeamCity has the ability to define the priorities of build configurations. We can configure these priorities from **Build Queue | Configure build priorities**.

This leads us to the **Priority classes** page. Apart from the existing classes—**Default** and **Personal**—we can create our own priority classes and assign a priority score to them. The score ranges from `-100` to `100`, with `-100` being the lowest priority and `100` being the highest.

We can create a new priority class, say `High`, by clicking on the **Create new priority class** button. We can provide a name and score for the new class and also add build configurations to the class. The following screenshot shows the `High` priority class, with the `deploy-to-test` configuration added to it:

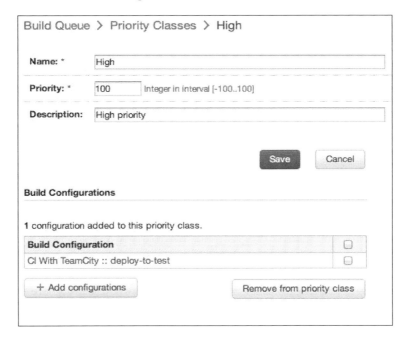

 Build scheduling in TeamCity is more complicated than the simplified explanation given here. Low priority builds that have been in the queue for a certain length of time can trump even high priority builds.

Interacting with TeamCity from build scripts

It is possible to send information (and commands) about the build from the build scripts to TeamCity. This information can be about tests, statistics, build status, and so on.

 More detailed information about build script interaction with TeamCity can be obtained from the documentation located at `http://confluence.jetbrains.com/display/TCD8/Build +Script+Interaction+with+TeamCity`.

This feature is especially useful when we are using a tool that is not (yet) supported by TeamCity, and hence we do not get the tight integration, such as information regarding the tests being run, and so on.

Such interactions from the build scripts to TeamCity can be done in two ways, which are discussed in the next two sections.

Service messages

Service messages are essentially pieces of text that are the output from the build script flowing into the standard output of the build process. Service messages adhere to a particular format expected by TeamCity, which, in general, is:

```
##teamcity[<messageName> 'value']
```

The `<messageName>` parameter is one of the predefined message types recognized by TeamCity, and `'value'` is the value for the particular message type.

For example, to set a custom build status message that can be used to convey more information about a particular run of the build, we can use the following service message:

```
##teamcity[buildStatus status='SUCCESS' text='{build.status.text}
Deployed build 1.0.10 to UAT']
```

 The `1.0.10` value, of course, will come from a property/variable/ parameter that is used by the build scripts.

This will update the build status message to show the extra information `Deployed build 1.0.10 to UAT`, as shown in the following screenshot:

 `{build.status.text}` is the status message set outside of service messages. For the build configuration shown in the preceding screenshot, it was the `Tests passed: 10, ignored: 1` message that was the value of `{build.status.text}`.

Similarly, there are many other predefined service messages to change the build number, change the status of the build, upload artifacts, report tests, update the progress of the build so far, and so on.

Creating teamcity-info.xml

The `teamcity-info.xml` file is an XML file that can be generated by the build script/build process to pass information and commands back to the TeamCity server. It is similar to service messages, except that the messages are collected in XML form and then automatically transferred back to the server.

The `teamcity-info.xml` file is expected to be generated in the root directory of the project and is automatically picked up.

 This method is deprecated, and service messages are the recommended approach for interactions between build scripts and TeamCity.

Service messages and `temcity-info.xml` enable the tight integration between the build script and TeamCity, which might not have been otherwise possible for tools not supported by TeamCity. Effectively, they expand the support of TeamCity to virtually any build tool and framework we may end up using.

Summary

Concepts like templates and Meta-Runners help in managing lots of build configurations without introducing duplicated settings. Artifacts and build history cleanup ensure that the TeamCity server can continue to run forever without having to worry about running out of disk space.

Commenting, tagging, and pinning builds help in improving the discoverability of builds and provide extra information about them. Service messages help us to integrate new and custom tools with TeamCity, thereby bringing them on par with tools that are supported out of the box.

Build queue priority classes help us to ensure that builds are scheduled in an efficient manner and are not starved of agents.

These advanced concepts help us in tweaking and fine-tuning TeamCity to a great extent, thereby making it all the more easy for us to set up a long-running and well-oiled CI process.

In the next chapter, we will take a look at what's beyond CI, enter the world of **Continuous Delivery (CD)**, and see how TeamCity can help us there too.

11

Beyond CI – Continuous Delivery

We had a quick introduction to **Continuous Delivery (CD)** in *Chapter 1, Introduction*. This chapter aims to expand on the concept and explores how a CD setup can be achieved using TeamCity.

First, we begin by looking at what CD is and why it is beneficial. Then we look at how the deployment pipeline can be configured in TeamCity so as to achieve these benefits of CD.

What is Continuous Delivery?

CD can be defined as the processes and practices through which applications are made available to be deployed to production at any time.

 A key thing to note here is that the applications are made available for deployment to production but are not necessarily deployed. Having every build of your application deployed to production automatically is called **continuous deployment**. With Continuous Delivery, the builds may be deployed to a **User Acceptance Testing (UAT)** environment so that the different stakeholders can try out the application and then make a decision to deploy to production.

CD is a natural extension of CI. In other words, CI is the base on which a CD setup can be built, and it is not possible to even start talking about CD without thinking about CI. While CI enables integrating code written by different developers, CD is about ensuring that that the code is available for deployment to production in a timely and reliable manner.

CD, hence, involves getting the artifacts of the integrated code and deploying it to various environments in succession to enable multiple levels of automated and manual testing.

Moreover, CD is as much about the tools and practices as the people involved. Communication and collaboration between the developers, testers, and business and operations is of paramount importance.

Why Continuous Delivery?

What is the need to have our software always ready to be deployed to production? Well, it enables us to test out new ideas and features as soon as possible. Code that is lingering in the repository without being used by the customers is of no use. In a similar vein, bugs in production can also be fixed pretty quickly.

Doing frequent releases to production also reduces the risk involved in releasing to production. A huge delay between releases leads to lots of changes happening in production at the same time. The risk of breaking things is very high, and the costs of finding and fixing the issues are high as well. It is also this risk and fear of doing releases that causes the divide between the development team and the operations folks or system admins. Frequent releases help in keeping the changes small, and issues can be isolated and fixed faster.

The deployment pipeline

We have addressed the what and the why of CD in the previous sections. This section answers the how.

The deployment pipeline is the central part of a CD setup. We have already implemented the core aspects of the deployment pipeline while implementing CI for various projects in the previous chapters. We take a look at the deployment pipeline in detail in this chapter, and how it can be configured in TeamCity.

 We will be looking at some settings and features of TeamCity that have already been covered in previous chapters so as to keep this chapter self-contained.

A typical deployment pipeline implementation is shown in the following diagram:

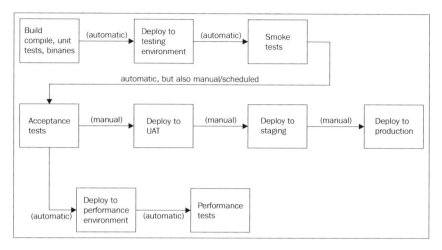

The pipeline has many sequential and some parallel steps. The code, and everything needed to have it running in various environments, is version controlled and progresses through these steps till it is finally deployed to production.

> Each step shown in the previous diagram generally maps to one build configuration in TeamCity. But, depending on the complexity of the setup and team preferences, a step in the diagram might even be a collection of build configurations within a project in TeamCity.
>
> Also, the exact steps, of course, will vary from implementation to implementation.

The initial step, marked as Build is triggered when developers check-in to the repository. It generally does the most basic steps of compiling the code (if needed), running the unit tests, and generating binaries, if any, as artifacts. The artifacts that are generated in this stage progress through the pipeline and are utilized in the different steps without having to be rebuilt.

> The Build step is not the only entry point for code. Functional test code changes can directly trigger the appropriate automated testing steps. Changes in the deployment code can trigger the deployment steps such as Deploy to testing. Configuration management and infrastructure code changes may update the environments.
>
> Moreover, not only code changes, but changes in internal and external dependencies, say, a new NuGet package being published, can also trigger builds.

The next step, `Deploy to testing environment`, deploys the generated artifacts to a CI environment. In the next two steps, we run **Smoke** and other automated functional tests against the instance of the app deployed in this CI environment.

We can think of these steps as being part of a standard CI setup, where the application is built, unit tested, and a set of automated functional tests is run against it. CI, hence, produces the artifacts that have gone through automated tests and are ready to be deployed to different environments (such as UAT, performance, preproduction, production, and more). On these environments, the application is put through more automated tests, for example, regression tests, manual tests, and also performance tests as required.

> Generally, some of the steps happen in parallel. For example, in the previous deployment pipeline diagram, performance testing is done in parallel to the UAT. Depending on the needs, the parallel steps may or may not merge back. In the Performance testing example, a build that fails the performance test may or may not be available for deployment to environments including production.

The artifacts are finally deployed to production and, hence, made available to the users. Any artifact that is available to deploy to production is known to have gone through the rigorous process of automated and manual testing.

Implementing the deployment pipeline in TeamCity

In this section, we will be looking at the different features that TeamCity provides for a proper CD and deployment pipeline setup. We will also be exploring how certain features encourage the best practices of CD, and some of the not-so-best practices.

A view of the deployment pipeline, visualized as build configurations and projects, is shown in the following screenshot:

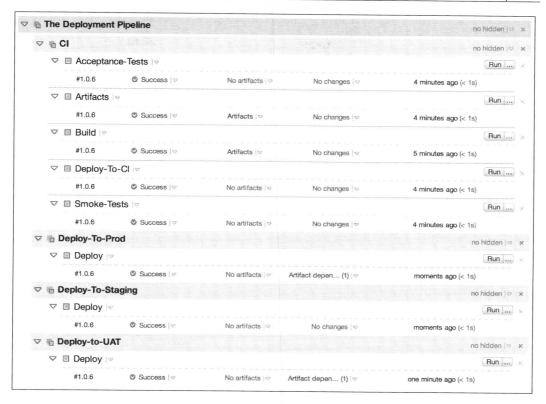

Here, the initial steps for a standard CI setup are grouped under the **CI** project. The steps to deploy to different environments (except for the CI environment) are moved to separate projects. Generally, deployments have multiple steps, such as deploying to multiple servers, running sanity tests after doing the deployment, and so on. This warrants separate projects for them.

Also, deployment to different environments needs to be managed through proper access control as it is not ideal to give everyone the ability to deploy to production or even the UAT environment. Apart from security and compliance, this can be for as simple a reason as avoiding accidents.

Publishing and consuming artifacts

It has been mentioned multiple times that one of the best practices of CI (and by extension CD) is to build our artifacts only once and use the generated artifacts for all the following steps.

The concept of artifacts (and artifact dependencies) in TeamCity enables this practice. We specify artifacts that are to be exposed from a build configuration in its **General** settings page, as shown in the following screenshot:

Build counter: * ⑦	7	Reset counter
Artifact paths: ⑦	Edit artifact paths:	
	artifact.zip	

Newline- or comma-separated paths to build artifacts. Ant-style wildcards like `dir/**/*.zip` and target directories like `*.zip => winFiles,unix/distro.tgz => linuxFiles`, where `winFiles` and `linuxFiles` are target directories are supported.

In the case of our sample deployment pipeline, we generate the artifacts in the Build step and need to expose the artifacts in this step alone. If we look at the CI project in the deployment pipeline in the TeamCity screenshot, however, we can see that there is also another build configuration named Artifacts, which also exposes artifacts. This is a dummy build configuration created just to create a logical endpoint for the CI process. The Artifacts build configuration just copies over artifacts from Build and exposes them again. The downstream deployment steps use the artifacts from the Artifacts step.

When the build is run on an agent, the specified artifacts are uploaded back to the TeamCity server and become available for downstream steps to use.

We can consume artifacts thus generated using the Artifacts Dependency feature of TeamCity. For example, the Deploy-To-CI build configuration has the following Artifact Dependency configured to fetch the artifact from the upstream Build step, as shown in the following screenshot:

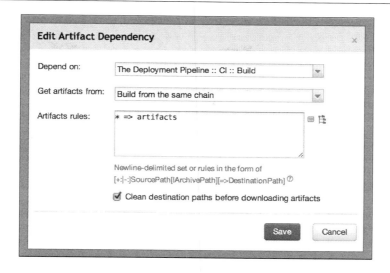

The **Get artifacts from** setting is set to **Build from the same chain**. This ensures that the artifact is fetched from a build from upstream in the same run of the build chain. We will be talking about build chains, and how to configure them, in the next section.

Build chain for CI

A build chain in TeamCity helps connect build configurations into a sequence of steps using the snapshot dependency feature of TeamCity.

The most important feature of snapshot dependency is that the dependent build configuration uses the same source materials as the parent. This ensures that all the steps in our build chain work off the same material and not the latest material at the time they were triggered.

 Here, we will set up a build chain for the steps in the CI project. Later, we will see why the deployment steps were not configured to be part of the build chain.

To link two steps in a build chain, we configure **Snapshot dependency** on the successor step. For example, the dependency setup of the `Deploy-to-CI` step is shown in the following screenshot:

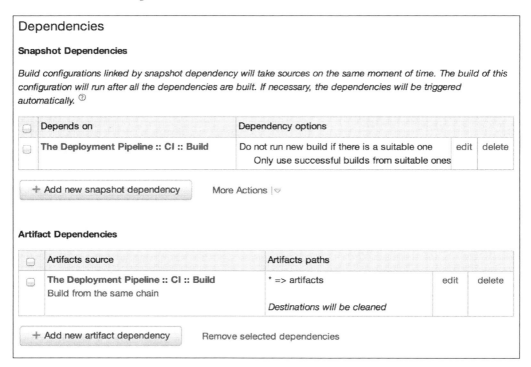

A part of the build chain so configured is shown in the following screenshot:

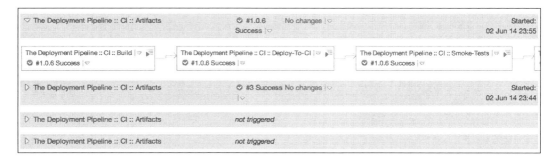

Going to the CI project page and clicking on the **Build Chains** tab brings up the build chain, as shown in the previous screenshot.

The initial step, `Build`, has a **VCS trigger** so that it can be triggered due to changes in the code. The configuration of this trigger is shown in the following screenshot:

 Similarly, other build configurations, such as `Smoke-Tests` and `Acceptance-Tests` can have their own VCS triggers to trigger them, in this case, switch on the changes to the automation tests codebase.

Between the build configurations in the build chain, we also configure **Finish Build Trigger** so that a build configuration can be triggered as soon as its immediate upstream build is done. The finish build trigger configured on the `Deploy-To-CI` build configuration is shown in the following screenshot:

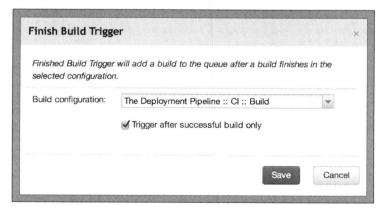

Deploying to environments

The build configurations to deploy to different environments are created in their own projects, as mentioned before.

The deployment configurations are not configured to be part of the main build chain. Working with snapshot dependencies is very restrictive in such cases. Usually deployment build configurations are fine with taking in the latest build and deployment code when they run as they (ideally) run off deployment scripts repository and not the main source repository.

Snapshot dependency triggers the upstream build if a downstream build is triggered. The selection on whether to trigger the upstream build is based on the VCS changes. If there are new changes, the upstream builds will be triggered. We don't want a new build to be triggered when we want to deploy to UAT. We want already generated builds to be deployed to UAT.

For these reasons, it is preferable to avoid snapshot dependencies and, hence, build chains, for deployment steps.

 Within the deployment steps to an environment involving multiple build configurations, say, deployment and then running smoke tests, snapshot dependencies, and build chains may be used. The recommendation is not to have them as part of a single build chain comprising the CI steps and the deployment steps.

We only add `Artifact dependency` so that the artifacts to be deployed are fetched.

Environments as gates

We want environments in our deployment pipeline to act as gates. We don't want to deploy to the staging environment without having deployed to the UAT environment and run the required tests (smoke, manual, and regression tests) against it. Similarly, we don't want to deploy to production without having deployed to staging.

With such requirements, we can configure the `Deploy-To-UAT` project's `Deploy` build configuration to have artifact dependency on the `Artifacts` build configuration. We can then configure the `Deploy-To-UAT` project's `Deploy` build configuration to expose the artifacts again. The `Deploy-To-Staging` project's `Deploy` build configuration will have an `Artifact Dependency` to fetch this artifact, as shown in the following screenshot:

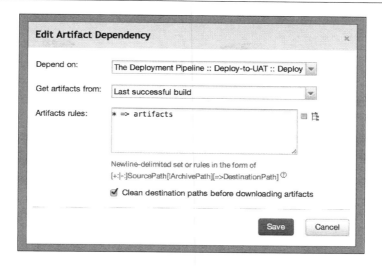

This way, only successful deployments to UAT are available as sources of artifacts for the staging environment.

Identifying the build that is deployed in an environment

It is very essential to quickly identify a build that is deployed to an environment. One of the easiest and quickest ways is to make use of the build numbers. The following screenshot show the build numbers of the artifacts deployed onto the different environments:

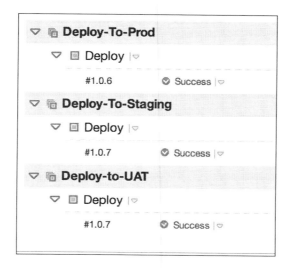

At a glance, we can see that staging and UAT have `1.0.7` deployed, whereas production is still on `1.0.6`.

We can configure this by first setting the build number to follow a release version pattern such as `1.x.x`. We set it in the `Build` step's **General settings**, as shown in the following screenshot:

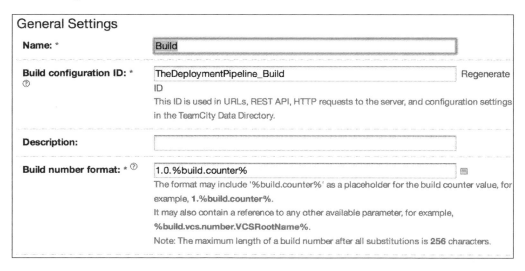

We then propagate this build number throughout the pipeline using the parameters provided by TeamCity. The build number of the build step is available in the `%dep.TheDeploymentPipeline_Build.build.number%` parameter.

The deployment build configurations can use a similar parameter for the `Artifacts` build configuration, as shown in the following screenshot:

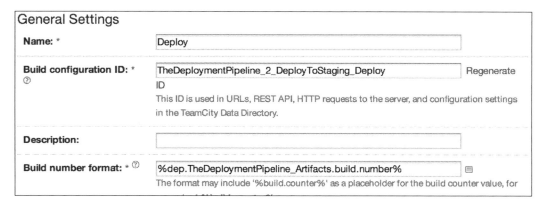

There are, of course, other ways to identify what build has been deployed to an environment. Hovering over the down arrow for the changes section in the overview page shows the artifacts dependency that was used, as shown in the following screenshot:

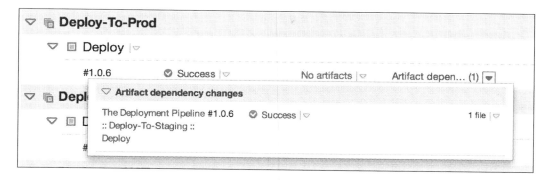

The same information can also be obtained from the **Changes** tab of a run of the build configuration.

Deploying any version to an environment

Deploying a given version to an environment is crucial for CD. We don't want to only deploy the latest builds. Also, at times, we want to rollback to a previous version.

Deploying any custom version can be achieved by using the **Run Custom Build** option, which can be reached by clicking on **...** (ellipsis) next to the **Run** button. The **Dependencies** tab of the **Run Custom Build** dialog is shown in the following screenshot with options to choose a version to deploy:

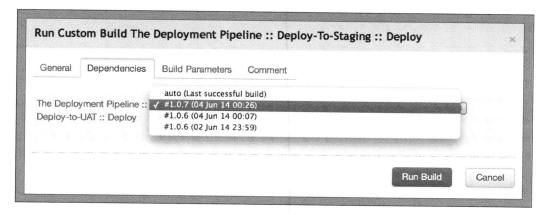

Another way that this can be done is using the promote build feature of TeamCity. Let's say we want to deploy a build that has been deployed in `Deploy-To-UAT`, to `Deploy-To-Staging`. We can go to the particular run of the `Deploy-To-UAT` and do **Build Actions | Promote...** to get the **Promote Build** dialog, as shown in the following screenshot:

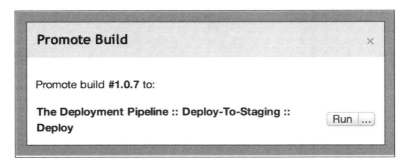

We can click on **Run** to promote this build downstream. We can also click on **...** to trigger the downstream builds while providing custom options.

Limiting deployment permissions to certain users

We generally want to limit the users who can deploy to different environments. It is recommended to create different groups for different environments and add the appropriate project-level permissions. To run the deployments, the project developer's permission is required as a minimum.

New groups can be created from the **Administration | Groups** page. Once a group has been added, we can add the roles from the **Roles** tab. For example, the roles of the **Prod Owners** group are shown in the following screenshot:

Passing sensitive information during deployment

There are many ways to handle passwords, keys, and other sensitive information that is required to run our applications in different environments. One approach can be to pass in these sensitive values as parameters through TeamCity.

The sensitive parameters can be added like any other parameters in the settings, but should be configured to be **Password** type if we don't want them to be displayed when we enter the value in the form.

The **Build Parameters** tab of the **Run Custom Build** dialog is shown in the following screenshot:

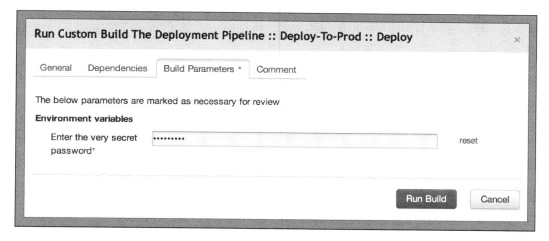

Feature branching and feature toggling

An important aspect of CD is to make sure that the software is deployable at any time. This means that work-in-progress features should not prevent it from being deployed. Feature branching and feature toggling are approaches to handle work-in-progress features.

Feature toggles enable us to switch off features that are still being developed so that the feature is not available to the end user even as we deploy code that contains the partially working feature. Feature toggles are also used to enable features only for a certain set of users so that a feature can be tested with that set of users before making it accessible to the whole user base.

Feature branching, on the other hand, involves working on a separate branch of the repository to develop a feature. The branch is not merged into the mainline until it is ready for release. While feature branching ensures that a feature can never affect production till it is fully ready, merging the branches back into the mainline might become tricky. This can especially be the case if the feature has been going on for a long time.

CI is about having all the developers commit to a single mainline (say, master on Git) and, hence, integrating their changes through an automated build and test process. Running builds with feature branches is, technically, not Continuous Integration and should be avoided.

Feature toggling is the recommended approach to ensure that work-in-progress features don't affect the ability of our applications to be released. Feature toggling is controlled mostly from the application side and is generally a runtime check. As such, TeamCity has no explicit support for feature toggles.

The ability to pass build parameters to a deploy build configuration while triggering it can also be utilized to pass feature flags to the environment while deploying. This is useful if the feature toggling mechanism for the application kicks in while deploying the code.

TeamCity, however, supports feature branching for the teams that do find it more beneficial than painful. The feature branching support in TeamCity allows us to alleviate some of the problems with feature branching, such as poor visibility on what's happening with the branch and its level of integration with the mainline.

The basic level of support for (feature) branches is through the **Branch Specification** setting of a **VCS Root**, as shown in the following screenshot:

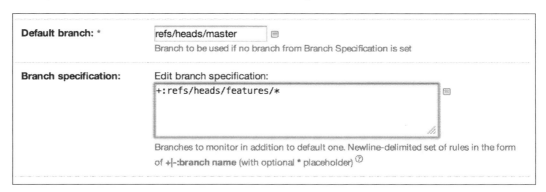

Here, the branch specification is given as `+:refs/heads/feature/*`, which configures TeamCity to build the branches under the features group.

When we configure additional branches like this, the **Default Branch** becomes important, as the default branch is the one that is used when a build is triggered manually just by clicking on the **Run** button in TeamCity.

The following screenshot shows how builds running off multiple branches are presented in the TeamCity web interface:

The `test-feature` branch is a branch that was created under `refs/heads/feature`. We can also filter the build results to show only a particular branch using the drop-down list in the top-left corner.

When working with feature branches, it is also possible to specify the branch, the build of which must be used while resolving artifact dependencies, as shown in the following screenshot:

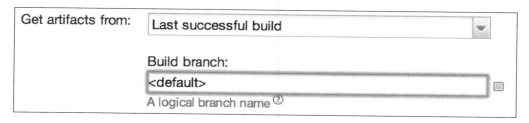

Summary

In this chapter, we delved into the depths of Continuous Delivery and how its core aspect—the deployment pipeline—can be implemented using TeamCity. We utilized TeamCity features, such as snapshot dependencies, artifact dependencies, promoted builds, run custom build, user roles and authorization, and so on, and saw how they help in creating an ideal CD setup.

In the next chapter, we will explore options to make TeamCity production ready.

12

Making It Production Ready

When we talked about installing and getting started with TeamCity, it was with the default setup. The default setup is great for trying out TeamCity, but it is not meant for production use.

TeamCity installation has to be tweaked to make it production ready. It has to be made reliable, secure, and ready to handle a large number of users, projects, and agents. In this chapter, we will take a look at some of the most important steps needed to make our TeamCity installation ready for the real world.

Using TeamCity with an external database

By default, TeamCity uses an internal database based on **HyperSQL DataBase (HSQLDB)**. The database files in the default setup are stored in `<TeamCity Data Directory>`, which is usually `<HOME>/.BuildServer`.

 HSQLDB is a database engine that provides in-memory and disk-based tables. More information about it can be obtained at `http://hsqldb.org/`.

While the internal database makes it very easy to evaluate TeamCity, it is not ideal for production usage. Heavy usage could result in loss of data and downtime.

The recommended way to use TeamCity in a production environment (read, real use) is to use an external database such as PostgreSQL or MySQL.

> TeamCity supports MySQL, PostgreSQL, Oracle, and SQL Server as it's an external database.

In this section, we will be using PostgreSQL as an example of an external database, and the steps that will be mentioned are similar for other databases as well.

Configuring PostgreSQL as an external database

Instructions to install PostgreSQL on various platforms can be obtained at `https://wiki.postgresql.org/wiki/Detailed_installation_guides`.

Once PostgreSQL is installed, we need to create a database and a user for TeamCity to use. This is done using the following set of commands:

```
$ createdb teamcity
$ createuser -PE teamcity
```

The first command creates a database named `teamcity`. The second one creates a user named `teamcity` and also prompts you to enter a password for the newly created user.

> Detailed and up-to-date information on setting up TeamCity to use an external database can be found at `http://confluence.jetbrains.com/display/TCD8/Setting+up+an+External+Database`.

Next, we use `psql` to issue queries to PostgreSQL, as follows:

```
$ psql
# grant all privileges on database teamcity to teamcity;
```

We use the `grant` query to grant all the privileges on the `teamcity` database to the `teamcity` user.

After the new database and the user are created, we can configure TeamCity to point to this database.

TeamCity has to be stopped before you perform the following steps. Also, after these steps are performed, old data will be lost. To preserve the existing data, follow the steps provided in the next section.

Before TeamCity can make use of a particular external database, we need to have the necessary driver through which TeamCity can talk to the database. The driver `libs` are to be put in `<TeamCity Data Directory>/lib/jdbc`.

We can download the appropriate JDBC driver for PostgreSQL from `http://jdbc.postgresql.org/download.html`. We have to ensure that it matches our version of PostgreSQL and JRE.

With the driver configured, we can point the TeamCity server towards our database. This is done via a `database.properties` configuration file, placed in the `<TeamCity Data Directory>/config` directory. The templates of this file are available for the supported databases in the same directory. We can copy `database.postgresql.properties.dist` as `database.properties` and update the properties as follows:

```
connectionUrl=jdbc:postgresql://localhost:5432/teamcity
connectionProperties.user=teamcity
connectionProperties.password=teamcity
```

 Here we assume that the database is on the same host as that of the TeamCity server. If the server is on a different host, `localhost` needs to be replaced appropriately.

With the connections file set, TeamCity should automatically set up and use the new database when it is started.

We can confirm that the server is using our external database by navigating to **Administration | Global Settings**, as seen in the following screenshot:

TeamCity Configuration	
Database:	PostgreSQL (user: teamcity)
Data directory: ⑦	/Users/teamcity/.BuildServer
Artifacts directory:	/Users/teamcity/.BuildServer/system/artifacts
Caches directory:	/Users/teamcity/.BuildServer/system/caches

The previous section talked about moving to an external database and starting with fresh data. It is also possible to migrate data from the internal HSQLDB to the external database (and even between different external database engines), which is what we will be looking at in the next section.

Migrating from one database to another

The `maintainDB.sh` (or `maintainDB.cmd`) script in the `<TeamCity Home directory>/bin` directory helps us to migrate from one database to another if we need to preserve the data in the internal database or even if we want to move from one external database to another (say, from PostgreSQL to MySQL).

To migrate the data from the internal database to our new PostgreSQL database, we can start by creating a `database.postgresql.properties` file (not the `database.properties` file) with the same database connection information as we saw in the previous section.

Now, we can run the `maintainDB` script as follows:

```
./maintainDB.sh migrate -T <TeamCity Data directory>/config/database.
postgresql.properties
```

The script migrates the data to the target database and also creates the `database.properties` file in the `<TeamCity Data directory>/config` directory so that the server can start using the new database.

We can start up the server and confirm that the data is preserved and also that it is using the new database.

Backup and restore

Taking frequent backups and the ability to restore them when needed is an essential requirement for any production system. In this section, we will talk about some of the strategies to back up and restore TeamCity data.

Taking backups from the server UI

Through **Administration** | **Backup**, we can take a backup of almost all the server-related files and data. The page to create backups from the TeamCity server UI is shown in the following screenshot:

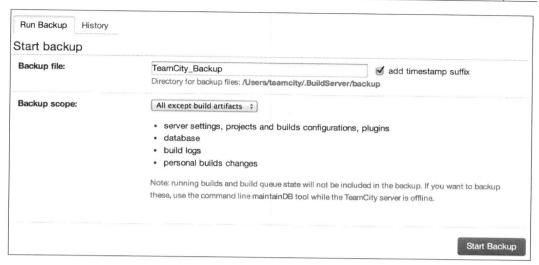

We can change the **Backup scope** option to include only Basic Data — the database and server settings, projects, build configuration, and plugins. This leaves out the build logs and personal build changes from the backup. We can choose **All except build artifacts** to back up all the data. There is also a **Custom** option available, where we can pick and choose the data to be included in the backup.

Clicking on **Start Backup** starts the backup process and creates the appropriate backup file in the location specified.

> The backup process can take a lot of time and uses server resources. It is hence advisable to perform back ups during low usage periods.

The ZIP archive created as part of the backup process can be used to restore the server anywhere — even in a different OS, using any (internal or external) database.

> While the backup can be taken using the server UI, it can also be initiated using the REST API.

The backed-up data can be restored using the `maintainDB` tool. We will be covering the usage of this tool for both backing up and restoring data in the next section.

Backing up and restoring data using the maintainDB tool

We have already used the `maintainDB` tool to migrate from one database to another. The same tool can also be used to back up and restore data.

The `maintainDB` tool can be used to back up all of the data, which is similar to the backup procedure of a web UI, using the following command:

```
maintainDB backup -C -D -L -P
```

The different flags to control which settings/data are to be backed up are given in the following table:

Flag	Backup content
C	Build configuration settings
D	Database
L	Build logs
P	Personal changes

> The flags that can be passed to `maintainDB.sh` can be learned easily by just running the script without any arguments.

The advantages of using the `maintainDB` tool over the TeamCity web UI option are as follows:

- The server need not be running when the backup is being taken. In scenarios where the server has stopped and a backup needs to be taken, this can be handy.
- While the online backup option doesn't include running and queued builds, having the server shut down ensures that all the builds are included (since, of course, no build is running at that moment).

Backups can also be restored using the `maintainDB` tool. An example command is as follows:

```
./maintainDB.sh restore -F <TeamCity Data Directory>/backup/TeamCity_
Backup.zip
```

Before you restore, the `<TeamCity Data directory>` directory needs to be cleared.

Like with the case of migrate, while restoring backups, we can also use the `maintainDB` tool to restore to a different database, including the internal one.

A manual backup

The final backup option is to manually back up the necessary part or all of `<TeamCity Data Directory>` and `<TeamCity Server directory>` as required.

A manual backup involves copying files and directories as needed, using appropriate tools such as `rsync` and so on. When using an external database, backup methods that are appropriate to the database must be employed. For example, in the case of PostgreSQL databases, the `pg_dump` utility may be employed. For uninterrupted backup solutions, DB replication strategies might have to be explored as appropriate.

Neither the server UI backup option nor the `maintainDB` option backs up the artifacts due to their sheer size. Backups for artifacts are necessary, for obvious reasons, and need to be done manually by backing up the `<TeamCity Data Directory>/system/artifacts` directory.

 It may also be necessary to back up agent data, especially the configurations located at `<Agent Home Directory>/conf/buildAgent.properties`.

Handling upgrades

Another important aspect of a production system is the ability to handle upgrades gracefully. The server should not end up losing data or be down for a long time because of upgrades.

When updates are available for TeamCity, the Administration pages show a notice to that effect along with a download link, as shown in the following screenshot:

Once the message is hidden (by an administrator), it can be accessed in the **Server Health** page under **Administration** along with other server-related messages.

The first thing to do before an upgrade is back up all the relevant data and settings. Due to the changes in the structure of the data, both in the data directory and in the database, most upgrades to newer versions of TeamCity will not support downgrades back to the older version. If we run into problems after an upgrade, the backups will turn out to be lifesavers.

Updating a server installed via an archive

Updating the TeamCity version for a server installed via an archive, as mentioned in *Chapter 2, Installation*, essentially involves replacing the old directory with the contents of the new archive.

The update mechanism doesn't work with existing files, and hence it is necessary to completely remove the existing files and copy over the files for the updated version. We can start by removing `<TeamCity Home directory>`, where the previous archive was extracted to, while installing TeamCity.

The backup strategy may not include <TeamCity Home directory>. While performing an update, it is recommended that you back up this directory before removing it.

The archive that contains the updated TeamCity version can now be extracted to <TeamCity Home directory>.

Any of the configuration files that were updated should be copied over to the new installation from a backup. It may be necessary to redo the changes rather than just copy the files over, as the files may have changed between versions. For example, if the TeamCity server port is changed through the <TeamCity Home directory>/conf/server.xml file, we need to ensure that the same change is done in the new installation as well.

Once the necessary files have been put in <TeamCity Home directory>, the server can be started. We can now continue the update process from the web UI.

The server will now enter the **maintenance mode**.

 A TeamCity server can enter the maintenance mode due to many reasons, but the most common is when the data format that it sees is not what's expected by it. In the case of an update to a newer version, this is, of course, expected.

The maintenance mode page, indicating that a data upgrade is required, is shown in the following screenshot:

T¢ TeamCity Maintenance

⚠ Data upgrade is required

TeamCity server requires technical maintenance. Please let the server administrator know this. ⓘ

I'm a server administrator, show me the details

TeamCity 8.1.3 (build 30101)

Clicking on the **I'm a server administrator, show me the details** link brings up the input to enter the authentication token, as shown in the following screenshot:

The token can be obtained from the server logs, located at `<TeamCity Home directory>/logs/teamcity-server.log`. Once the token is entered, the server will perform the data directory and database updates, as needed.

If everything goes fine, we should now be updated to the new version of TeamCity!

Updating TeamCity using the Windows installer

Updating TeamCity via the Windows installer is straightforward. After the necessary backups are taken, the Windows installer for the newer version can be run. It automatically uninstalls the existing version and installs the new one.

 We still need to redo any custom changes that have been done to the server configuration manually.

Once the installation is done and the server service is up and running, the server enters into the maintenance mode and the update can be finished by entering the token found in the server logs, as described in the previous section.

Updating the agents

One of the nice features of TeamCity is that the server automatically updates the agents. When a TeamCity server is updated, all the agents that are connected to the server are updated automatically. This is very convenient, as we don't have to worry about preserving the existing properties, configurations, and so on.

If we want to update the agents manually, say, due to an error in the automatic update process, we can get the Windows installer or the new archive for the agents and install them manually. These installers can be downloaded from the **Administration** page by clicking on the **Install Build Agents** link, as shown in the following screenshot:

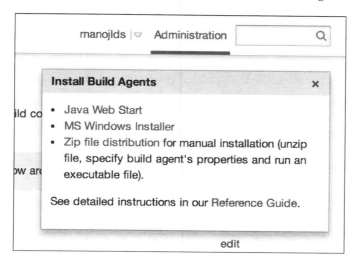

Just like the server installation process, care must be taken to ensure that custom configuration changes are carried over.

Monitoring resource usage, performance, and logs

Monitoring the resource usage and performance of any system in production is key to the long-term reliability and uptime of that system.

TeamCity provides administrators with many features to monitor the overall health of the server. We will be looking at some of these in this section.

Disk space usage

From **Administration | Disk usage**, we can have a look at the disk space being used by the server. This page provides a quick view of the available space for artifacts and logs and how much of it is being utilized, as shown in the following screenshot:

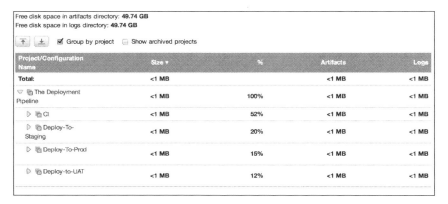

The page helps us identify which projects and build configurations are churning out large artifacts and logs, and hence we can tweak the artifact, log, and history cleanup accordingly.

 Build cleanup was discussed in *Chapter 10, Taking It a Level Up.*

It is also possible to go even deeper into individual build configurations and see how many builds and artifacts are being retained along with the cleanup policy in effect, as shown in the following screenshot:

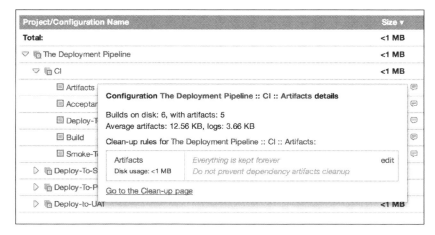

TeamCity server diagnostics

The **Diagnostics** page under **Administration** provides a detailed overview of the performance of the TeamCity server. From this page, it is possible to get information on memory usage and JVM settings for the server and also access the server logs to identify issues, if any.

A view of the **Diagnostics** page is shown in the following screenshot:

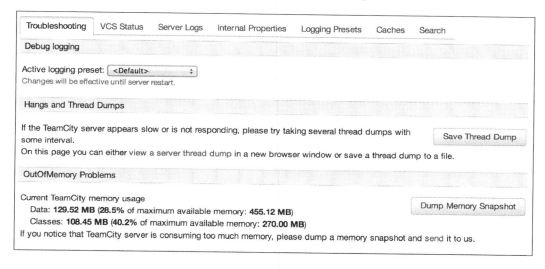

From the **VCS Status** tab, we can see how many VCS roots are being polled and also see how long the polling process is taking. This helps us identify slow VCS roots that may be degrading the performance of the TeamCity server as well.

The **Server Logs** tab gives us access to all the logs from the `<TeamCity Home directory>/logs` directory. From the **Internal Properties** tab, we can have a quick look at the properties defined in `<TeamCity Data directory>/config/internal.properties`.

The **Logging Presets** tab allows us to take a look at and add new `log4j` logging configurations. The **Caches** tab lists caches created by TeamCity. Finally, the **Search** tab shows the statistics of the index and the search process.

Tweaking the TeamCity JVM

TeamCity is a JVM application, and its memory usage can be tweaked like any other JVM application. For large production uses, the defaults may not work, and hence a few tweaks in the heap and PermGen memory allocated to TeamCity may be needed.

Much of the tweaking can be done by passing the appropriate flags, `-Xmx` (heap space) and `-XX:MaxPermSize` (PermGen space), to the JVM.

There is no *one size fits all solutions* here. The exact values to be used will vary from installation to installation based on usage, number of build configurations and projects, and so on. It is recommended that you use a minimum of 750m for the heap space (`-Xmx750m`) and 270m for the PermGen space (`-XX:MaxPermSize=270m`) and then raise it from there as needed.

These flags can be passed to the JVM used to run the server using the `TEAMCITY_SERVER_MEM_OPTS` environment variable.

> If TeamCity runs with a 32-bit JVM (the default through a Windows installer), it is limited to 1.2 GB of heap memory. If it is deemed that more memory is needed, TeamCity should be switched to a 64-bit JVM, and we should start with at least double the memory than before (`-Xmx2500m`).

Summary

In this chapter, we discussed the configuration options and features that help in making TeamCity a reliable CI server in production use.

Using an external database, backing up TeamCity data frequently, and looking at the diagnostics information provided by TeamCity can result in a stable server that can run day in and day out.

TeamCity is a feature-rich tool, and it only keeps on improving with every new release. Its high-fidelity support for different tech stacks, ranging from Java to Node.js, should be evident from the chapters that cover these topics. The well-thought-out features of TeamCity, its strong community, and growing number of plugins make it ideal for any situation, workflow, and team.

With this, we come to the end of the book, but not our journey with TeamCity as a CI and CD tool. The features that were introduced and the steps that we covered should lay a strong foundation to perform CI and CD for both small and large teams alike.

Index

P

parameters 57-59
pending changes
  checking for 187
performance
  monitoring 245
  TeamCity server diagnostics 247
Phanthom.JS 152
plugins
  URL 13
PostgreSQL
  configuring, as external database 236, 237
PowerShell 125
PowerShell-based build tools 125
PowerShell build runner
  used, in TeamCity 125-127
practices, CI 8
Pre-tested (delayed) commit 160
Private Key setting 47
project
  building 86, 87
Project Monitor
  about 171, 172
  URL 171
Project Object Model (POM) 85
projects
  build configurations, hiding 178, 179
  hiding 178
  navigating across 179, 180
projects of interest
  managing 177
project statistics 67
promoting 205
Psake
  URL 125
pull requests
  about 166
  build status 166, 167
  reference link 167
  setting up 166
Push URL setting 46
Python build runner
  building with 150, 151
Python runner plugin
  installing 149
  URL, for downloading 149

PyVirtualDisplay
  URL 59

R

Rails
  about 129, 134
  installing, Blunder used 131
Rake 132
Rakefile content feature 134
rbenv
  about 130
  URL 130
  used, for installing Ruby 2.0.0-p353 130
rbenv-gemset plugin
  URL 130
rbenv, preferred over RVM
  URL 130
rbenv rehash command 131
regular expression (regex) 168
Remote Run 159, 160
Remove finished build permission 207
reports
  publishing, as artifacts 64
Report tabs 66
Resolve field
  options 181
resources types 68
resource usage
  disk space usage 246
  monitoring 245
restore 238
results actions
  building 202
  commenting on 202, 203
Robolectric
  URL 142
Ruby 2.0.0-p353
  installing, rbenv used 130
  installing, RVM used 130
ruby-build command 130
Ruby interpreter
  setting up 136-138
Ruby Make. *See* **Rake**
Ruby on Rails. *See* **Rails**
Ruby Version Manager. *See* **RVM**

Thank you for buying
Learning Continuous Integration with TeamCity

About Packt Publishing

Packt, pronounced 'packed', published its first book "*Mastering phpMyAdmin for Effective MySQL Management*" in April 2004 and subsequently continued to specialize in publishing highly focused books on specific technologies and solutions.

Our books and publications share the experiences of your fellow IT professionals in adapting and customizing today's systems, applications, and frameworks. Our solution based books give you the knowledge and power to customize the software and technologies you're using to get the job done. Packt books are more specific and less general than the IT books you have seen in the past. Our unique business model allows us to bring you more focused information, giving you more of what you need to know, and less of what you don't.

Packt is a modern, yet unique publishing company, which focuses on producing quality, cutting-edge books for communities of developers, administrators, and newbies alike. For more information, please visit our website: www.packtpub.com.

Writing for Packt

We welcome all inquiries from people who are interested in authoring. Book proposals should be sent to author@packtpub.com. If your book idea is still at an early stage and you would like to discuss it first before writing a formal book proposal, contact us; one of our commissioning editors will get in touch with you.

We're not just looking for published authors; if you have strong technical skills but no writing experience, our experienced editors can help you develop a writing career, or simply get some additional reward for your expertise.

Jenkins Continuous Integration Cookbook

ISBN: 978-1-84951-740-9   Paperback: 344 pages

Over 80 recipes to maintain, secure, communicate, test, build, and improve the software development process with Jenkins

1. Explore the use of more than 40 best of breed plugins.

2. Use code quality metrics and integration testing through functional and performance testing to measure the quality of your software.

3. Get a problem-solution approach, enriched with code examples for practical and easy comprehension.

Hudson 3 Essentials

ISBN: 978-1-78328-055-1   Paperback: 124 pages

Get Hudson 3 up and running on your system quickly and easily

1. A practical guide that will teach you how to deploy Hudson 3 on an open source application server.

2. Run Hudson 3 in standalone mode for testing and evaluation.

3. Learn how to build, test, and deploy your applications with Hudson.

jQuery UI 1.10: The User Interface Library for jQuery

ISBN: 978-1-78216-220-9   Paperback: 502 pages

Build highly interactive web applications with ready-to-use widgets

1. Packed with clear explanations of how to easily design elegant and powerful frontend interfaces for your web applications.

2. A section covering the widget factory, including an in-depth example of how to build a custom jQuery UI widget.

3. Revised with updated code and targeted at both jQuery UI 1.10 and jQuery 2.

jQuery UI Cookbook

ISBN: 978-1-78216-218-6   Paperback: 290 pages

70 recipes to create responsive and engaging user interfaces in jQuery

1. Packed with recipes showing UI developers how to get the most out of their jQuery UI widgets.

2. Solutions to real-world development issues distilled down in a reader-friendly approach.

3. Code examples written in a concise and elegant format, making it easy for the reader to adapt to their own style.

Please check **www.PacktPub.com** for information on our titles

Made in the USA
San Bernardino, CA
26 December 2015